Airborne to the Mountains

Airborne to the Mountains

by
James Mills

New York: A. S. Barnes and Company, Inc.
London: Thomas Yoseloff Ltd.

To
Warwick Deacock, Donald Kinloch, and Derek Pritchard

Foreword

It is a criticism often leveled at those who explore and climb mountains that they make the narrative of their adventures so objective, so ordinary sounding that the uninitiated reader, avid to share the experience, feels cheated of the lure and excitement of the unknown. That this should be so is understandable; it is a part of the make-up of most explorers that they shun sensationalism. There is everything to be said for modesty in the telling of an adventure, and against any tendency to compete with the drama and emotionalism of fiction.

But to understate the facts and still more, to conceal feelings actually experienced and expressed is a disservice to literature. What is more, it tends to be dishonest, by presenting only half the truth. If, in fact, a story of mountain exploration is worth the telling, then let it be told fully, frankly, and subjectively.

This is just such a story and I, for one, welcome this book of the adventures of four young men in Alaska, bent on exploring the glaciers and making new ascents of peaks in the region of Mount McKinley. Their achievements, commendable as they were, are less the focus of interest than the effect of hardships imposed on them by a combination of the country, the climate, and their own burning sense of mission. The physical strain, the emotional tensions, the disappointments and moments of triumph; the touches of human squalor amid the pure beauty of the mountain scene:

7

these impressions register in the reader's mind and affect his own emotions more deeply than the mere narrative of events.

The size and nature of the cast for this story contribute to these effects. Much has been said about the merits of "small" expeditions and the evils of "large" ones; I have sometimes detected the flavor of "sour grapes" in these dissertations. Yet I have never met the climber who, consulting his own personal preference alone, would not opt for the small group of trusted companions for a mountain journey. But aside from the practical reasons which call for a larger group in order to fulfill a given task, it is often overlooked that the larger expedition makes for easier human relations. To carry out a plan of mountain exploration involves the division of a large expedition into small groups; but the stresses and strains in these groups tend to be less than in the case of a small expedition because the sense of isolation is less and reserves of strength are close at hand. There is, so to speak, a larger human cushion on which to fall back.

Having had experience of many mountain expeditions of varying sizes, I can vouch for the authenticity of the difficulties revealed so candidly by Jimmy Mills in this book. It is the more to the credit of himself and his party that emotional molehills were not mistaken for mountains and that the real mountains were, as they have always been for those who frequent them, the means of unity between four enterprising, very different and individualistic young men.

Sir John Hunt

May 26, 1961

Acknowledgements

The success of most expeditions stems as much from the months of careful preparation as from the actual work in the field. During this crucial period, in which the idea is translated into the action of planning and organization, the leader and his party depend greatly on those few sponsors and patrons who, like them, believe the expedition to be worthwhile. This need was considerably greater with a pioneer venture in two fields, military and geographical.

We were extremely fortunate in those to whom we turned for support, and I am greatly indebted to Major General R. N. H. C. Bray, CB, CBE, DSO; Brigadier M. A. H. Butler, CBE, DSO, MC; Major General D. S. Gordon, CBE, DSO; Sir John Hunt, CBE, DSO; Mr. L. P. Kirwan, CMG, TD; Major General W. H. D. Ritchie, CB, CBE; and Mr. Bradford Wasburn, for their advice and confidence and for the time they gave on our behalf.

I would also like to express my gratitude to the Mount Everest Foundation and the Parachute Brigade for their generous grants in aid, and to Mr. George Greenfield and Mr. Patrick Matthews for their assistance in making the Expedition possible financially.

The Canadian Army did much to ease the problems of our journey through Canada and in doing so enabled us to balance the fine calculations of our dollar account. As always their hospitality was magnificent. In particular I wish to thank Major General J. P. E. Bernatchez, CBE, DSO, CD;

Brigadier H. L. Meuser, OBE, CD; Colonel G. F. Stevenson, CD; Lieutenant Colonel E. G. Shannon, OBE, CD; Major Bryce Gillis; Major J. C. Wilson; Captain S. McLeod; Captain J. Campbell; and the sole British representative, Major G. Storey, of my own Corps.

For the generous assistance of Mr. Bud Geer, of Northern Freightways, and Mr. P. Loiselle, while we were in Dawson Creek, I am also extremely grateful.

Without the immense and versatile support of the United States Air Force in Alaska, the Expedition might not have been possible; certainly we could not have fully achieved our aims. To Major General Bennet, Colonel Conley, Colonel Sawtelle, Lieutenant Colonel Riechert, Mr. Scott Heater, Major Stewart, Captain Coile, and Captain Weatherwax, who were chiefly instrumental in organizing and carrying out this support, I am deeply indebted. I would ask them to accept this expression of gratitude on behalf of those other members of the United States Air Force who contributed so much to the success of the Expedition.

Two members of the Royal Air Force, on the staff of Headquarters, Alaskan Air Command, Squadron Leader G. F. Daly, DFC, and Squadron Leader E. W. Cropper, shared with their United States Air Force colleagues responsibility for making the arrangements for air support and many other facilities while we were in Alaska. I thank them both.

Robert Elsner, Keith Hart and Lieutenant Bob Raethle found time, during the preparations of their own expedition, to give us valuable mountaineering advice and assistance with our last minute needs. To them and Fred Milan, also of the Alaskan Alpine Club—for his counsel and memorable hospitality—I am extremely grateful.

The use of helicopters ultimately insured that the Expedition was able to spend the maximum time in the mountains and, in consequence, on its program. For permission to employ helicopters I am indebted to Mr. Grant Pearson, whose co-operation was an important factor in the planning.

I am most grateful to the Norwegian Army for the loan of equipment and to the British manufacturers who provided food, clothing, and equipment free or at reduced costs. Together they helped to lighten the dragging weight of the financial millstone, which is, unfortunately, a traditional piece of neckwear for expedition leaders.

My thanks are also due to my wife and Miss Anne Buckman who typed and checked the original manuscript and to Mrs. Priscilla Fleming who drew the maps.

Finally, I must express my gratitude to the members of Expedition who permitted me to draw fully upon their diaries, provided photographs, wrote appendices, and gave advice on the writing of this book.

Contents

List of Illustrations

The following illustrations appear as a group after page 132.

Airborne to the Mountains

"So far as I can venture to offer an opinion on such a matter, the purpose of our being in existence, the highest object that human beings can set before themselves is not the pursuit of any such chimera as the annihilation of the unknown; but it is simply the unwearied endeavour to remove its boundaries a little further from our little sphere of action."

—Huxley

1. *The Idea*

In 1954, while serving with the Parachute Brigade in Egypt, I led a small expedition to Ruenzori, the Mountains of the Moon. By virtue of assistance from the Royal Air Force and free travel as armed guards on the Kenya railway, we kept the total cost per head down to £60. One of the more significant aspects of the expedition was that the R.A.F. made it possible, flying us five thousand miles from Fayid to Nairobi, and return, for a charge of a mere fifty-seven shillings.

Expeditions are an expensive business, and outside England most parties are heavily supported financially by grants from government sources and scientific bodies. Expeditions from the British Isles, however, have been a matter for private enterprise, and were so even before the days when Shackleton was forced to lie in wait at rich men's doors, in the hope of obtaining money for his Antarctic schemes. In this post-war world, the aspiring explorer would not only be hard put to discover a wealthy benefactor to waylay, but he would also find that the cost of financing expeditions has risen steeply.

The only hopeful sign in this frustrating situation was the formation of a trust fund from the proceeds of the successful 1953 Everest expedition, for the purpose of assisting mountaineering expeditions. Even so, more expeditions foundered for lack of funds than ever left these shores. The success of our own small venture to Ruenzori had been encouraging, and it had also given me an idea. If the services, with their vast resources, with their own air and sea routes crossing the world, could be persuaded to support such expeditions—thus taking the place of the old private backer—then a great many things would become possible. They would, however, only become possible for officers and men in the forces; but there were signs that this kind of extramural activity would be looked upon benevolently from the heights of Whitehall. After all, in more spacious days there had been a well-established tradition of soldier explorers whose journeyings, financed largely from their own purses, had also been viewed with favor by the hierarchy. Now, in a more confined era, I planned to continue this tradition with the approval and, what is more, the practical support of the War Office.

In times of peace a watchful Treasury inhibits the soldierly tendency to treat money as currency. I knew, therefore, that War Office enthusiasm for any scheme I might put forward would be tempered by Treasury caution. Obviously, my proposed expedition must, in the very nature of things, labor under all the disadvantages of a pioneer venture; but I intended that by its success it would convince the War Office and the Treasury that this sort of activity was worthy of their wholehearted support, and that without it the spirit of adventure and enterprise in the army would be denied vital and useful expression. The expedition would also be a pioneer one in another equally important sense. I wanted to break new ground for British mountain exploration, to get away from the well-signed and familiar path which leads to the foot of the Himalayan peaks. I wanted to grapple with new problems; follow unknown paths; to gain experience for future mountain journeys in Asia and Antarctica. I wanted to struggle for the prize, to extend myself intellectually and physically, and above all to measure myself against the mountains of my own desire.

2. *The Planning*

I REMEMBERED that in one of Mr. Eric Shipton's books he had, while making plans for future exploration, considered the mountain ranges of Alaska. Some research at the Royal Geographical Society revealed that no British expedition had visited the area. In fact only one British climber, Dr. Graham Brown, who was a member of an American expedition which had climbed Mount Foraker, had been into these mountains at all.

The area which lies in and around the McKinley National Park, two hundred miles west of Fairbanks, seemed to offer the best opportunities for exploration. Most of the activity had been concentrated on the massive 20,300-foot pile of Mount McKinley, which dominates this uplifted wilderness of ice-sheathed mountains riven by vast glacial chasms. The region to the south of McKinley and the great Muldrow Glacier which is sustained by it was largely unknown and was most easily accessible from the north.

Wonder Lake, which possessed an airstrip and could be gained by the road from McKinley Park Station on the Anchorage-Fairbanks railway, was the obvious jumping-off point. From here it was possible to use pack-horse transport for crossing the morass of the tundra to McGonagall Pass. The other method, less expensive but distinctly more arduous, was to relay food and equipment by back-packing. It would be a time-consuming and unrewarding labor. Apparently air drops were often used to support expeditions, but these were sanctioned by the Park Authorities only when expeditions had a scientific purpose.

High winds, heavy snowfalls, sudden storms, and low temperatures were the main climatic features. No porters were available; and it seemed that once in the mountains for a protracted stay, one must supplement the techniques of a climbing expedition by the methods of arctic travel.

I now had a good idea of the problem and a skeleton of the requirements on which to plan, but a mass of information was still required from someone who knew the region. From my research I had discovered that Mr. Bradford Washburn, of the Museum of Science in Boston, was the undoubted authority on Mount McKinley and the man who could probably provide the answers to my questions. In early March, 1955, I wrote to Washburn and sent him a lengthy questionnaire. So began a correspondence which lasted for twelve months, a correspondence which placed at my disposal all Washburn's vast experience. Without his help the expedition might not have taken the field.

After much careful thought about the size of the party, I came to the conclusion that four men was the minimum number for safety in the mountains and the maximum number for which we were likely to get free service air passages. In the event of our not getting any service assistance, the total cost of the expedition would be about twelve to fifteen hundred pounds. I then put forward my plan, which embodied a request for four free return air passages to North America and three months' leave with pay, to my Brigade Commander, Brigadier Gordon. With characteristic and practical enthusiasm he endorsed my proposals and sent them to the War Office.

Having thus received some measure of official approval, I applied to the McKinley Park authorities for permission to undertake the expedition. A few weeks later Grant Pearson, the Superintendent, replied, granting permission. He also posed me another problem. The Park Regulations ruled that all expeditions going into the area must have a stand-by rescue party. He suggested that I try the United States Air Force in Alaska, who had their own rescue teams. It seemed a rather forlorn hope that my letter to the U.S.A.F. Commander, Alaska, would bear fruit. To my surprise this reply came within a month, confirming that a stand-by party could be provided and advising me to arrange the details with the R.A.F. officer on his staff, Squadron Leader Daly. I could hardly believe that on the basis of a single letter, this considerable assistance (which later on was to be greatly increased) could be given so easily by a foreign service to one officer in another!

By this time I had selected, from the members of the Brigade mountaineering club, the three men who would form the rest of the party. Captain Warwick Deacock, of the Middlesex Regiment, now in Second Parachute Battalion, was to be the second in command. He was a fortunate choice. My posting to Germany had been fixed for the end of the year, and I wanted someone who would be able to share the weight of the planning as well as negotiate with the War Office in my stead. This latter aspect was important; for the other two members, being national service men, had not the experience or the seniority to handle what might prove to be the most difficult part of the organization. Warwick Deacock, aged 29, was a big man, six feet three inches tall and dark-haired. He was a regular soldier and had been a Marine Commando. After joining the Royal Marines in 1944 he served four years until his release in 1948. He then spent the next few years in civilian life, in jobs ranging from laboring, and

truck driving on the Continent, to being a sales representative
of a stationery firm in London. In 1951 he applied to join
the army, coming back to service life as a regular officer. He
had ski-mountaineered in Japan, instructed in Army winter
warfare schools, and climbed in the Austrian and French
Alps and on rock in Britain.

Donald Kinloch, the doctor of Third Parachute Battalion,
was 26 years of age. He had served in the army just a year,
being a graduate of Glasgow University, where he was a
member of the mountaineering club. Tall, fair-haired, and
strongly built, he had probably the most ice and snow experience in the party. His record of climbs covered Yugo-
slavia, the Swiss and French Alps, Norway, the Pyrenees,
and his own beloved Scottish crags.

The youngest member, aged 23, was Derek Pritchard, also
an officer in the Third Parachute Battalion. Short and power-
fully built, he was a student artist before being called up.
His experience covered the Swiss and French Alps and he
had done a good deal of rock climbing in the Lakes and
North Wales.

I was 29 and a regular soldier in the Royal Army Service
Corps now serving as the Brigade M.T.O. I first joined the
Army in 1944. My service had been broken by a year in public
relations in the city, before I returned to the Army in 1949.
In 1950 I had been a member of an expedition to Norwegian
Lapland and four years later had led the Ruenzori party.
My other climbing experience included the mountains of
South Sinai and rock in the Gold Coast and North Wales.

In our spare time we worked hard on the organization of
the expedition. Jobs were allocated, equipment and food
lists drawn up, and we held frequent coordinating conferences. In addition to my own flourishing correspondence
with Bradford Washburn, McKinley Park, the United States

Air Force, and the War Office, begging letters—the symbol of postwar expeditions—began steadily flowing out to firms from whom we hoped to get food, equipment, and clothing, free or at concessional rates. Expedition planning and organization must be efficient, meticulous, and flexible. The 1953 ascent of Everest had shown the value of army staff methods in tackling the problem. We, too, used this approach. The basis of success in the field is always laid in these months of hard exacting work before departure.

The official wheels began to grind slowly at the War Office. By late September we were informed that we had been granted three months' leave with pay (hitherto unheard of except for national expeditions) and that application had been made to the Royal Canadian Air Force for our air passages. To give ample time for them to investigate the possibilities, as well as to allow a maximum of planning time, I fixed the date of departure for late April or early May. This meant that we would arrive in the mountains during the last few days in May, having missed, perhaps, a month or more of the best weather. Our withdrawal, therefore, might be hampered by bad conditions, but the first priority was to have sufficient time in which to organize the expedition.

During a visit to the Scott Polar Research Institute we were lucky enough to meet someone from Alaska who knew the mountains. He was Fred Milan, an American anthropologist from Fairbanks; in 1954 he had been on McKinley during the rescue of an injured climber. Milan was able to give us a great deal of first-hand information and suggest useful contacts. He was a short, thickset man, of ageless appearance, and possessed of a striking personality. We were to see more of him, rather unexpectedly, later on.

In December, after I had been interviewed by the Committee of the Mount Everest Trust, the expedition received

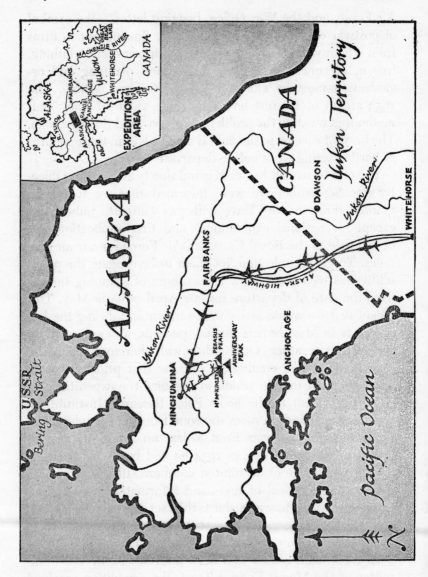

a grant of £350. With our own contribution of £240 we now almost had sufficient funds if—and it was a big If—the Canadians provided our transport across the Atlantic.

Later in December, tragedy almost overtook the expedition, when Warwick fell a hundred feet while climbing in North Wales. He was saved to some extent by his second, who broke his thumb in the process, but he did, nevertheless, hit the ground very hard. In good parachutist style he landed feet first, his shoulder harness, as opposed to a waist loop, keeping him upright. His back was badly damaged, including some crushed vertebrae, and he had internal injuries. It says much for his toughness and resiliency of mind that not only was he able to walk away from the accident, but throughout the long weeks in hospital and convalescence he continued to work hard on the expedition.

Early in the new year, with the assistance of Washburn, I completed the final plan for our work in the field. Our aims were now firmly fixed as follows:

1. To explore the Traleika Glacier system and to attempt unclimbed peaks around it.
2. To carry out a program of medical and physiological research.
3. To make a geological collection for the United States Geological Survey.
4. To carry out a program of meteorological observations.
5. To test service equipment, clothing, and rations.
6. To make a film record of the expedition.

On January 8 I left for Germany, leaving my wife to face another two months' separation before joining me.

The day after my arrival I heard over the wireless that the First and Third Parachute Battalions had been flown to

Cyprus. With Donald in Cyprus, Warwick in Aldershot, Derek now a student in London, and myself in Germany, the organization of the expedition became even more difficult, and inevitably a heavier burden fell upon Warwick.

Meanwhile, my correspondence with Squadron Leader Daly in Alaska had progressed well. Not only was our stand-by party assured, but verbal agreement had been given for us to be accommodated at Fairbanks and to be flown in from there to Wonder Lake.

As the days dragged on, our travel arrangements made no apparent progress. Files grew fat with letters in spite of the fact that Warwick and I now spoke to each other on the telephone at least twice a week. We were reluctant to give up the hope of Canadian assistance, yet with the passing of the days the chances grew slimmer. The anxiety of wait·ing, and the tension induced by argument and counterargu-ment in countless letters, slowly climbed to a pitch. Towards the end of January we finally learned that the R.C.A.F. could not assist us. This news cleared the vagueness which had been inherent in all our planning. We must now pay our own way and find the money to do so. As a first step we raised our own contribution to £500. It was not easy.

With the help of a literary agent, whom I knew, and some businesslike work from Warwick, the remaining money came rather more easily than we had expected. In return I was to write a book—which I had intended doing anyway—though I now had to work to the publisher's timetable. George Green-field, our agent, saved more money for us, by persuading the Rank Organization to give aid in kind in the form of film. We on our side agreed to provide the camera and make a record of the expedition.

It was a relief to be free of uncertainties and when War-wick managed to get us berths on the *Neptunia*—a Greek Line boat leaving Southampton for Montreal on May 5—we knew for the first time that the expedition would take place.

At last I had some firm dates on which to work and I sent a proposed itinerary of our journey to everyone from the War Office to Headquarters Alaskan Air Command. At Easter, Warwick, now completely fit again, came to stay with Jeanne and me in Germany. After months of writing and telephone conversations, this meeting proved invaluable.

A few days before I left Germany there was a minor shock. Derek contracted chickenpox, which unfortunately prevented him from receiving valuable instruction from the Rank Organization. More serious was the possibility that we might need a new member, but fortunately there was just sufficient time left in which he could recover.

On April 26, at lunch time, I walked into Second Parachute Battalion mess to find an anxious Warwick talking hard into the telephone. The call was from the War Office asking me to go there the next day to give certain guarantees concerning the finances of the expedition. Fortunately I was able to do this. After a busy day in London I returned to Aldershot to find Donald in the mess, having returned from Cyprus a week before. Derek had also arrived.

In the evening we went to the Medical Inspection Room where Donald examined us all thoroughly, then inoculated and injected with the usual ghoulish enthusiasm of an Army Medical Officer. He seemed rather disappointed that we were all quite so healthy.

The remaining week was probably the most harrowing of the whole organization period. There seemed to be a never ending trek from one office to another, and multifarious tasks to be done, ranging from collecting rations to collecting visas and dollars. On one day the four of us were spread between North Wales, Somerset, and London.

On Friday we met together in George Greenfield's office to draft out a legal agreement on the financial aspect of the expedition, with special regard to shares in possible profits on the book, articles, and lecture rights.

Later that day, after a final interview with the publisher,
I met an agitated Derek for tea in Piccadilly. At the last moment his camera had been found unsuitable for taking film
onto which a sound track would be dubbed; it was too slow.
Our contract with Rank's was at stake, with embarrassing
possibilities for George Greenfield and the expedition. I
turned on Derek furiously. We had already passed through
one crisis involving the camera, when the owner had asked
for it to be returned, Derek having forgotten to tell him for
how long we required it.

"Why didn't you check this before? You've had the blasted
thing ages."

"I thought it was all right."

"You didn't check it then?"

"Well . . . no. Not until now."

"You are a bloody idiot! You realize we might fall down
on our contract and be made to look like complete fools."

"I realize now, but it didn't occur to me. . . ."

We left the tea shop and walked down Piccadilly while
Derek explained that one of the Rank staff had given him
the address of a well known camera shop in Montreal. The
man at Rank's had promised to write to the proprietor and
ask him to hire us a good cine camera at a reasonable price.
This appeared to be a solution, but I pointed out that it
would cost us more money, which we could ill afford. We
parted at the tube station, not the best of expedition friends.

That night there was frenzied session of packing and it
was two-thirty on Saturday morning when we closed the last
box and labeled it. At eight-thirty the same morning—the
fifth of May—we were on the docks at Southampton, bleary-
eyed and excited at the thought that we were at last away
after all the months of anxiety and frustration. I thought of
the five hundred or more letters which lay in files as eloquent
evidence of a part of the effort needed to achieve this day.

3. The Journey

THE DOCKS were lifeless; the *Neptunia* was delayed outside the harbor by fog. Towards midday, after a long tedious wait, our boredom was relieved by the sight of the ship sliding alongside the quay. It was an undistinguished vessel already crowded with immigrants from Europe. We were through with the formalities fairly early; the customs, having been forewarned, were extremely helpful.

The queue of passengers dragged its way on board, and at two o'clock we found cabin 135, well down in the ship in an ovenlike atmosphere. We retrieved our boxes, kitbags, sacking parcels, and the one vast shapeless sack full of boots and rope—which fitted perfectly the name Quatermass—and somehow stowed them into the cabin. All was complete except my ice axe, which had been left securely fastened to my kitbag. I discovered that it had been dropped over the side by one of the loaders.

The ship sailed an hour later. No one showed any elation at the fact that we were at last on our journey; we were all too tired. But here we were, crammed together in a tiny cabin with forty-odd pieces of baggage. Our acquaintance with each other was of not more than a year; we had never climbed together; and for the last few months we had been separated over Europe, England, and the Middle East. Now for three

months we were scarcely to be out of each other's sight. I
lay on my bunk wondering how the party would knit together in these first few days and later in the mountains.

Mercifully, for I am a bad sailor, the sea was calm, and
after tea we wandered around the decks looking over the
ship and our fellow passengers. There were not more than a
dozen other British people on board. The majority were immigrants to Canada from almost every part of Europe, with
a sprinkling of people from all over the globe. If the atmosphere and the passengers were cosmopolitan, then so was
the ship. Presumably, it was Greek-owned, but hailed from
Bremen with a mixed compliment of Germans and Greeks;
it was registered in Panama. An old ship, solidly built and
slow, its arrival date in Montreal was May 15. The food was
good with several courses to the meals, which were served
swiftly, if without finesse, one knife, fork, and spoon sufficing
for each meal. Our table companions, a New Zealander, an
Austrian, a South African, and two Irishmen, ate voraciously
—as did Warwick and Derek—but Donald and I were beginning to feel the effect of the now lively sea. Soon after
dinner we went to bed, falling to sleep quickly in spite of the
appalling heat.

The weather continued stormy and the sea rough. The
Neptunia wallowed, pitched, and rolled, on its slow way west-
ward. It was as well that the voyage was a long one. There
was a good deal to do. We packed rations, checked equipment, practiced our crevasse technique, and began a series
of tests to initiate Donald's medical program. When these
tasks had been completed, we held daily conferences at
which one part of the expedition's program was discussed
and explained, with the object of ensuring that everyone
was thoroughly conversant with all aspects of the work.

Well before we reached Montreal we had become good

friends, and I was confident of the party's ability to achieve success. The time had now come when orders were unnecessary and I no longer had to give the lead. A great many expeditions have been spoiled by leaders who were too conspicuous in their desire to command. Mountaineers are noted individualists and any attempt to give orders is often sharply repudiated. On any expedition each man must have his own job: there should be no spare men. Each man then feels he has a stake in the expedition, and a personal responsibility for its success.

We now not only knew what we were to do individually, but also the full scope of the expedition work and the details of each man's particular function. There remained for me the task of making a "tactical" plan for the actual ascents and journey in the mountains. This, of course, would be subject to any additional information and guidance I might receive from Bradford Washburn. I also had to act as spokesman in dealing with other services and officials.

The point I am trying to stress is that we were a team; yet we were also very much individuals, going to the mountains for different reasons, but with a common desire to achieve the expedition's aims. Obvious and heavy leadership in such a venture would be disastrous.

Rough seas delayed our arrival for at least 24 hours, but at last, on the sixteenth, we saw the coast of Newfoundland and that night anchored in the channel at Quebec. The next morning the immigrant authorities and travel agents had come aboard, and the ship was alive with people rushing from table to table gathering pieces of paper. We bought our train tickets—saving money by traveling immigrant class—and in the afternoon went ashore into Quebec. Near the station our cinema-trained ears heard the sound of an

engine whistle, wailing its hornlike note—a sound redolent
of the West, and the days when the line was being pushed
across the buffalo-filled plains. It was like a welcome.

The multicolored cars fascinated us with their enormous
length and power. With their yawning grilles there seemed
to be more risk of being devoured by them than knocked
down. There was, unfortunately, very little time and after
a visit to a bank we returned regretfully to the ship and a
step test ring-mastered by Donald.

At eighty-thirty the next morning we posed in a slightly
embarrassed manner for a cameraman, before being ushered
through the Customs by a member of the British Army Staff
in Ottawa and Major Gillis of the Canadian Army. Outside
the shed, two large, black, chauffeured cars swept us away
from the dockside. Warwick and Derek headed in the direction of the camera shop, armed with a letter from Rank's,
while Donald and I were driven to the Army headquarters
in Montreal.

The others appeared just before lunch with the news that
they had made arrangements to hire, for $150, two 16-mm
cameras, plus three lenses. On our return we had the option
of buying one, less the hire fee. I was delighted, and Derek
appeared rather more cheerful about the filming now that
the stigma of the camera problem had been removed. We
had lunch with the G.O.C. General Bernatchez and were
cheered to discover that the Canadian officers on the spot
were willing to assist us in every way.

The afternoon found Warwick and Derek closing the deal
at the camera shop, and Donald and myself being shown
the sights of Montreal from the Mount Royal. We all met
together at the station and were whisked in one hour at great
speed to Ottawa. With a dollar a day each to spend on
food, we decided to try our luck at getting a cheap meal outside the hotel. We wandered through the city, touring the

cheapest eating places, comparing prices, until we found what we thought was suitable. The proprietor watched fascinated while in his broken-down cafe we searched the menu for the most at the least, with Donald offering advice on calorific and vitamin values, while Warwick, who held the purse, muttered cautionary financial statements. We finally settled on the soldier's favorite—fish and chips—for sixty cents each.

Back at the hotel we held a conference on the next day's program, then Warwick and I went down to the bar. It was Albuhera day, the most famous of Warwick's regiment's battle honors. As we raised our glasses to the toast I reflected on the rather bizarre situation. The bar was dimly lit and grimly functional, illuminated only by lights behind the bottles and the television eye above us. In the dim recesses of the room sat the morose drinkers, and in the corner two drunks slumped over their tables, while in the center two British drank to a battle fought in an obscure Portuguese village over two centuries ago. It seemed ritualistic, like dressing for dinner in the jungle. A cynic would have smacked his lips at the sight.

The next morning at six I was off to the airport for the journey to Boston. It was just before noon when I arrived. In the airport lounge I was met by Bradford Washburn, a small, spare, sandy-haired man, with a determined set to his features. He is the undoubted authority on the McKinley region, and has dedicated a considerable part of his life to the study of the mountain in all its aspects, including the survey of the area. Over lunch we began to talk about the expedition plans. He soon confirmed my hopes of the Traleika Glacier system by pointing out on the map six peaks which were unclimbed. Three of them were unnamed. I asked if he thought it possible to cross the cirque which enclosed the head of the glacier and gain the unexplored Eldridge Glacier area on the other side. Washburn was doubtful. There was very little information on the cirque and no air-photograph coverage, but he thought that at least from one side it would rise very steeply from the glacier. In addition to these unclimbed peaks, there was an unseen col or two to be attempted, an outside chance of finding a new route up McKinley, and of course, the exploration of the Traleika.

Back at Washburn's office, overlooking the harbor, we examined more air photographs and he briefed me on the geological work. The flight back to Ottawa was smooth and uneventful. My visit had been eminently successful; in these few hours more had been achieved than in weeks of correspondence.

The following afternoon we left Ottawa and began the train journey across the continent. My impressions of the five days of rail travel are of prairie spreading to the horizons, grain elevators flicking by, meals of bread and cheese, uncomfortable nights huddled in our seats, the pall of smoke from forest fires shrouding the sky over Edmonton, and the violent swaying and jolting of the eccentric North Alberta Railway's train as it blithely clodhoppered its way north, as though happy to be escaping from the timetable-encompassed world of the great transcontinental lines.

As we alighted from the train at Dawson Creek station, we were greeted heartily by an ebullient character who introduced himself as Captain Scotty McCleod—a member of my sister corps the Royal Canadian Army Service Corps. After the introductions, our kit was loaded into a station wagon and we were whirled off in a large car to the garrison mess. From the well-stocked bar he dispensed a rugged and generous hospitality. In spite of our protests we were not released until the last possible moment. After an alarming fifty-mile car journey, up the gravel-surfaced Alaska highway, we reached the airfield at Fort St. John with a few min-

utes to spare. There was just enough time to unload our
stores from the station wagon, which had preceded us, and
get them weighed. The heat, the speed of our journey, and
the beer combined to exert their influnce on us, and it was
four tired and deliberately steady British officers who
boarded the aircraft. We took off and flew north with the
arctic light streaking the sky. It was a smooth, pleasant
flight broken by only two stops. I sat drowsily watching the
mountains below us, like pale ghosts in the grey light. The
wingtips seemed to touch the phosphorescent rim of the
sky.

Whitehorse was a cluster of lights crooked in a bend of
the river below a high cliff, and we descended slowly to the
airfield on the heights. Again we were met by a Canadian
officer, who took us to our quarters where we fell into bed
thankfully.

We arose late and wandered round the town, sightsee-
ing and shopping. Log cabins and shacks crowded against
large modern concrete buildings. Sleek modern cars stood
in the potholed dusty roads nosing the wooden sidewalks.
It was a town of contrasts and character, still pervaded by
the atmosphere of the Service sagas and the days of the gold
rush. In several shops complete prospecting outfits could be
bought, and through the streets roamed unkempt huskies.
At street corners small listless knots of Indians, clothed in
the garb of the white man, stood talking, idly scuffing the
dust with their feet. On the river bank sat the great white
steamers, which once had been the only means of communication during the summer months. Here they rested, relics
of those early days when men had flooded to the north to
seek elusive fortunes—hulks in which lights once glowed
and music sounded, lying mute and divorced from the moving life of the waters. One there is, which in a single journey, with a cargo of women and whisky, had made its owner

a fortune. It has lain there since, a symbol of those roaring days.

As we took off from Whitehorse, into the pale glow of the northern night, I was becoming conscious of a growing excitement. This really was the last lap. I looked upon Fairbanks as a sanctuary where problems would not touch us. The idea of this expedition I had carried in the citadel of my mind for over a year. It had withstood the shock of disappointment and frustration, and the siege of nagging worry and anxiety. Now I longed for the peace of the mountains and the challenge of a different kind of struggle. Fairbanks seemed to represent a pause and a retreat; a chance to escape from worries and to free our minds in readiness for the mountains.

Below, range after range of mountains reached into the sky; glaciers, like wrinkled roadways, wound through them. The plane droned on in the faded light. I thought I recognized Big Delta and Fort Greely and my excitement mounted. The long descent began and then the bump of wheels and the runway racing by. The plane swung around outside the airport building and stopped. We filed slowly out of the aircraft door down the steps, with flashbulbs popping and photographers running to and fro, crouching to take shots. It was some time before I realized that we were their target. A voice called out my name and I turned to see an R.A.F. squadron leader on the other side of the barrier. The pattern of events was almost complete, and we were on the threshold of the mountains.

4. The Fly-In

AGAIN THE customs examination was merely a formality, arrangements having been made by the United States Air Force. We were then released to meet Squadron Leader Eric Cropper (Daly's successor) and Colonel Hubbard, the chief operations officer of the base, who welcomed us to Ladd Air Force Base. While we murmured sweet nothings about our journey, two of the air force public relations sergeants took more photographs from every angle.

"Shake hands with the colonel, Captain."

"Say, look this way, Captain. That's fine."

"O.K., relax."

We moved outside, made sure our kit was in an accompanying truck, and then followed Cropper in the direction of Ladd.

We crossed the outskirts of Fairbanks and drove on through the base gates. It seemed to stretch for miles on both sides and was quite the largest airfield any of us had ever seen. The car came to a stop to give way to a flight of black, red, and silver jet fighters which screamed in to land on a vast carpet of runway to our right. We motored on, catching glimpses of tall buildings and enormous hangars, into what seemed to be the center of the base where large blocks clustered around a meeting of roads. At one block,

signed Murphy Hall, the car stopped and the driver told us
that this was the bachelor officers' quarters. Inside, in a hall
complete with television set and a reception desk like a hotel, we again met up with Cropper. At the reception desk a
board on the counter announced that "Jackson R. Glantz
is your clerk for the night." Jackson was in fact a sergeant,
but we thought the idea rather friendly. We were shown up
to our room and after a wash and having turned off the
stifling central heating, we joined Cropper to stroll round
to the canteen, the officers' club being closed.

The canteen was rather like a N.A.A.F.I., but ten times
more expensive-looking and very chromium plated. At the
tables lounged soldiers and airmen and a good sprinkling of
officers and noncommissioned officers. Most of them were
dressed in dungarees or sweat shirts and in one corner a
multicolored juke box thumped out a tune. Our appearance
in Service dress, Sam Brownes, and red berets caused some
interest. We walked through feeling rather overdressed and
alien. As we queued up at the resplendent counter a soldier
sidled up to Cropper and tapped him on the shoulder. "Say,
chief, what outfit are you guys in, uh?" With a polite smile
Cropper explained our ranks and why we were here.
"Thanks chief, that's interestin'," said the inquirer and returned to tell his friends. Cropper said, "You know, I'm just
getting used to it—it's quite extraordinary at first."

At a table, over coffee and sandwiches, we talked generally about our journey. Later, back in our room, Cropper
briefed us on the set-up at the base and the program for the
morrow. We talked on until late and it was one o'clock the
following morning before we drew the curtains to shut out
the pale light and went to bed.

At eight o'clock we were talking to the Base Operations
Officer, Captain Coile. He was a short, round-faced man
with a bristling crew cut. We listened, fascinated by his

slow, drawling, Mississippi accent, as he described his reconnaissance flight out to the Wonder Lake strip that morning. The spring break-up was in full swing and the snow
was so mushy that no landing would be possible there for
some time. As we gathered around a large wall map he
pointed out an alternative airstrip at a lake called Minchumina, some 200 miles northwest of Fairbanks. Minchumina
was over 60 miles away from the fork of the Traleika and
Muldrow glaciers, 40 miles farther than Wonder Lake, the
point which we hoped we might reach by air. Now, Henry
Coile made his main point: as Minchumina was the only
strip available and the journey on foot across 60 miles of
sodden tundra was out of the question because of time, then
we must use a helicopter to get in. Because of this fact a
helicopter of the Air Rescue had been released for us. But
he said, "These chopper boys are mighty cagey. They're
scared of turbulence which occurs near the mountains, especially in the afternoons, and if it happens—why they'll just
dump you and you'll have to walk. Anyway let's go see
them."

Colonel Reichert, the Squadron Commander, met us in
his office and we sat down around a table with Coile, Cropper, and some other members of his headquarters staff. He
was a very large, friendly man with brilliant blue eyes, and
he radiated confidence. I felt that if anyone could get us
into the mountains it was this man. He came quickly to the
point.

"Now Captain, just run over your problem again and tell
me what you'd like us to do." I explained that we had a
heavy program of work and could not afford the loss of time
which the unrewarding relaying of stores across the tundra
would impose. Every mile flown nearer the glacier would
give us more time in the mountains. I quit the table and
walked over to a large relief map propped against the wall.

Someone handed me a small pointer. As the others swiveled in their chairs to get a better view of the map it suddenly came to me how much like an airborne assault this operation of the fly-in was becoming. I felt like a force commander briefing the pilots after their own people and the meteorology man had finished their part. I pointed out the fork of the Muldrow and Traleika glaciers as the place to which we should like to be flown, and indicated Cache Creek and the McGonagall Pass as a good line of fly-in.

Colonel Reichert pondered for a moment and then said, "Well look, Mills, I'm not promising anything, but we'll get you as near the goddam glaciers as the weather and safety will permit."

He turned to Coile, "Now operationswise what's the plan?"

Coile said, "Colonel, if these boys load their kit along with the chopper gas in the C-47 tomorrow afternoon, we can take off at 0600 on Friday. The chopper can take off earlier and arrive at Minchumina before us. I guess we can get the first load away in the chopper at about eight o'clock."

Reichert nodded agreement. "O.K. I'll fly the SA-16 over to cover the chopper." He turned to me. "That suit you, Mills?"

I said that it was just fine. It was as easy as that. This casual use of three aircraft staggered me. The smooth, quick decisions were to me, a regulations-haunted British officer, almost unbelievable. I looked at Warwick and he, too, seemed to be in the same state of unbelieving surprise. Then suddenly, at that point, I realized that Grant Pearson, the Park Superintendent, did not know of this plan to use a helicopter, and in any case he might want to exercise his right to inspect our equipment. I told the Colonel this, try-

ing delicately to put the point that Pearson might say no
or impose a delay in order to get a ruling from his chief.

Reichert was imperturbable. "O.K., if this guy gets awkward we may have to accept a delay, but anyway we'll help
all we can in getting you boys in. Now about the rescue
cover. We'll fly over once every three days and talk to you
on the radio. I'll give you a little URC4 set for that."

I was appalled. Think of the expense! No, surely we
couldn't accept this, it was too generous. "Really, Colonel, once a week would be enough. I mean . . ."

"Nope. We'll look in every three days—it'll be no bother.
What else can we do?"

The generosity was too much. I was weakening under the
impact. *Could I ask, in addition to all this, for a special
drop? It was pushing it rather but . . . there was the mail
. . . they had to come over anyway.* "If it's not too much
trouble, when you come over could you drop in air mail?"
I asked rather weakly.

"Sure, we'll fix that."

The chance was lost. I cursed myself; they would have
gone along with the drop. British reserve and American generosity had defeated me. I was to regret it later, in terms of
days lost to us. It was possibly my major mistake in the
whole expedition, although I was too overwhelmed with
events to realize it at the time.

The conference broke up and we left for lunch at the
field ration mess. Here Cropper and the four of us were
joined by Scott Heater, who was in charge of the Arctic
Survival Training School. His job was to train aircrew in the
art of survival in the event of their being forced down in the
wilderness. He was a tall, lean, rangy man with features
etched in rugged lines. His walk was almost a long-legged
lope and he seemed, to me, to be the epitome of the West-

ern backwoodsman. A deep soft voice completed the picture. I am sure that had Hollywood discovered him, Mr. Gary Cooper and others would have found his box-office appeal extremely competitive. He was very interested in the expedition—especially in our food. During lunch he kept Donald closely engaged, and their friendship was sealed when Donald discovered that Heater's grandparents were Scots.

From Cropper I learned more about the versatility of the Air Rescue Squadron. Besides their main role of rescuing the survivors from U.S.A.F. crashes, they took on an astonishing variety of tasks. They had rescued stranded Eskimos adrift on ice floes, evacuated whole communities threatened by the floods of the spring break-up, air-supplied families that were otherwise cut off, and found and rescued civil bush pilots when their only reference was an area of hundreds of square miles. In doing so they had developed techniques and procedures which must be second to none. I began to see why our operation had presented so few problems to Colonel Reichert.

After lunch I met Major Stewart, the acting commandant of the United States Army Arctic Indoctrination Center at Fort Greely. He would be in charge of the team of paramedics and climbers who would provide our rescue cover and I briefed him closely on our plans. Now all was tied up except for permission from Grant Pearson, and very soon I was talking to him on the telephone. Despite my very earnest pleading he refused to give a decision on the use of helicopters until Friday afternoon, the twenty-fifth, when he would come to inspect our equipment and rations. Somewhat gloomily I told Colonel Reichert, who agreed to stand down until Pearson gave us his answer. We could only wait. I kept telling myself not to worry, but every delay and problem ate into my reserves of patience.

Before I left the office I asked one of the staff officers if it might be possible to deviate from our line of flight on the way to Minchumina, and perhaps get a preview of the mountains and take some cine shots from the air. He thought it could be arranged.

The next morning, just before nine, I paid a routine visit to the headquarters. Just as I was leaving one of the staff said, "Oh yeah, I almost forgot, there's a couple of iron birds waiting for two of you for a flight over the mountains." I translated iron birds correctly as aircraft and equally non-chalantly said we'd go over to the squadron. With Derek and camera I went to the squadron office where we were kitted up. In the crew room I was introduced to Bob Raethle who was to be my pilot. We walked out onto the sunny tarmac of the runway and climbed into a jet fighter standing ready. After an unnerving briefing on emergency drills, my bewildered thoughts were roughly scattered by the wild scream of a siren. Raethle's voice came through on the intercom, "This is an alarm Jim, you'll have to get out." I pushed back the cover and heaved myself out onto the wing and as I dropped to the ground someone took my place. Around me, airmen were running in all directions and as I reached the crew room the first three fighters were racing down the runway, the sun dazzling on their silver skins. They were followed by flight after flight until the dust-filled air quivered with the scream of jet engines. High above, in the blue, vapor trails began to form heading for the north. Derek and I handed our kit in and were told to come back after lunch.

We had lunch together with Bob Elsner and Keith Hart, with whom I had corresponded during the planning, and also Bob Raethle. They told us about their plans for the ascent of McKinley by a new route up the steep and extremely exposed Pioneer Ridge. They hoped to do the climb in about a month and would enter the mountains a week after us. We formed an instinctive liking for them and they were unstinting in their advice and help. They also gave us canes for our route flags and put their own cars at our disposal. From Bob Raethle we received a connoisseur's opinion on the wear for glacier travel in hot sun: "Why, just a string vest and pants under my windproof suit, with my flaps open to let the air circulate."

At two o'clock Derek and I were back in the aircrew room dressed in our flying suits. Another quick run through the escape drills and the cockpit cover slammed to. The aircraft rolled forward, the jets screaming. A halt at the end of the runway; the checks with control; and the fighter surged forward along the black tarmac carpet. The speed of our climb crushed me down into the seat. I felt breathless, my body and arms heavy. I sat there with this stifling force upon me watching the red-and-white disc of the oxygen flow indicator flicker back and forth, showing each breath I took. We leveled out and the weight was withdrawn. There was no sound or vibration, only a feeling of complete steadiness as we rode forward, aloft on the invisible thrust of the jets. Bob's voice came through the intercom. "We're heading for the Rock Pile—that's McKinley—but it looks a little clouded in."

Ahead, a white wall of cloud stretched before us and we climbed above it, moving steadily over the sea of soft, billowing vapor. Below us it gradually shredded into wisps trailing like windblown veils. Beyond were the mountains. I checked the map on my knee and—yes, down there was the Muldrow, a grey wrinkled pathway, streams bleeding from its snout. We turned, sliding down, and in the ease and power of airy flight I forgot my purpose and sat engrossed in the scene below. It looked amazingly like the air photographs I had been given by Washburn, and utterly remote from my speedy world in the sun-dazzled perspex globe.

We sped up the Traleika, with moraines seaming its face, and then around the western buttresses of McKinley. A shout from Bob and below us I saw Derek's plane flashing past, minute against the enormous wall. There came to me the sudden realization of the majestic, forbidding vastness of these mountains. The starkness of their challenge burst in upon me, violating the security and warmth of my transparent cocoon.

"We're going round the mountain."

"O.K."

We banked to the right and gradually hauled our way round the enormous bulk of the mountain. On the other side was the terrifying downward plunge of the Wickersham Wall; its 13,000 feet entirely dwarfed our speed and we seemed only to drift past it. The avalanche-torn slopes and ice-fluted faces swept by in a frighteningly beautiful panorama. We dropped down fast, turned over the lower glaciers, and raced up the fretted knife-edge of Pioneer Ridge, then pulled up in an effortless curve over the summit.

Our speed was too great to note any one detail and it was too dangerous to fly low in the glacier canyons, for fear of the sudden pull of a downdraft. For a last few minutes we danced and pirouetted on wingtip, swooped and climbed over the vast areas of glacier and snow, split and racked with rock. The earth swung and tilted, rushed towards me, the detail of its surface becoming clearer with alarming speed, then dissolved, in a flash of a silver wing, into the blue, cloud-wisped sky. My limbs felt weightless and then lead-heavy by turns and in the circling kaleidoscope of heaven and earth I lost all sense of the plane's forward motion. So we mocked the mountains, scorning their challenge with airy flight, yet feeling the brooding enormity of their presence and recognizing that they still possessed the power

to destroy us. They demanded our respect. We turned away
into the clouded blue, the grandeur and magnificence of the
scene filling my mind.

The sharp pain in my ears, as I sat crouched in the seat,
made the descent to Ladd seem agonizingly slow and I was
highly relieved when we came to a halt on the runway. I
met Derek in the crew room and found that he had been
equally impressed and awed by the mountains. He had also
managed to shoot quite a considerable amount of film. He
was cautious about the result but excited over the possibility of recording something of what we had seen.

The next morning we were up early and I arranged my
own kit as a specimen—rather like an army kit layout—
for Grant Pearson to see. We also had on show a tent, some
rations, stoves, and other odd items, including the 8-foot
pole which the regulations required for searching for crevasses. Pearson and Keith Hart arrived very early and
rather unexpectedly. His first words were that the use of
helicopters was O.K. as far as he was concerned, and within
five minutes he had inspected our kit and pronounced himself to be delighted with it. He was a thickset, weather-
beaten man, in late middle age, with a delightful air of simplicity about him. Before he left we talked a while about
his journey to McKinley, some years before, and of his life
in the great park. He was obviously very much in love with
his work—a dignified, uncomplicated man living simply
and remotely in the wilds to which he was dedicated.

When he and Keith had gone I telephoned Colonel
Reichert and Henry Coile and was told to load our kit at
four that afternoon. Takeoff would be at six the following
morning. From Scott Heater we obtained the sledge, a spare
packboard, a nylon rope, and a long, heavy ice axe for myself. When all our equipment was assembled in the operations office it weighed just about a thousand pounds. We

kept with us our packboards and personal kit, plus enough equipment, including a tent and food, to keep us self-sufficient for a short time should anything go wrong with the airlift.

That evening was a stag night at the officers' club and for two dollars a head we could eat as much as we liked. We settled down to what was for us an expensive feast. Most of the rooms in the club, including the bar, would have done credit to any West End hotel. The acceptance of this standard was a matter of course to the Americans, but to us this luxuriant setting amid a wilderness of tundra—and just south of the Arctic Circle—was little short of unbelievable. We wondered how hard the Russians were living, just across the Bering Strait, and what they would think of this.

These Americans were here in the North and in many other parts of the earth like the new Romans, standing guard for the world against the modern barbarians. For me, this base symbolized all the surging virility of the American nation with its superb confidence in the power of machines and in its own seemingly boundless potential of men, brains, energy, and materials. The brash confidence in their way of life, which annoys their detractors and draws from the Old World men and women eager to become part of it, was abundantly in evidence.

The two-hundred-mile flight to Minchumina was uneventful and we dozed in the bucket seats, our feet up on the drums of gasoline and piles of our kit lashed to the aircraft floor. Occasionally we glimpsed far-off moutains. At 7:30 the Dakota came in low over the lake and touched down on the rough dusty strip. Already waiting there were the helicopter and the twin-engined amphibious SA-16. In the sunlight of the fine windless morning we unloaded the food and equipment and stacked it near the helicopter.

Colonel Reichert came down out of the SA-16 and greeted us. "Looks as though we've got a fine day for it, and the earlier we start the more chance we've got of getting you boys in."

He then briefed us on how to use the small square URC4 radio, with which we were to speak to the aircraft. We were also given two spare batteries and a waistcoat with pockets in which the radio and a battery could be carried. I handed over the extra seven pounds weight to Warwick, who un-characteristically seemed keen to carry it. Using a pile of ration boxes as a table I briefed the helicopter pilots, by air photographs and map, pointing out that if they could not get us up to the glacier, then it was possible to land in Cache Creek. The chief pilot, Captain Nolan, said, "Well, we'll treat this first flight purely as a reconnaissance and we'll take just two of you and about 200 pounds of kit. We'll try and get you in as far as we can, but this first try may take upwards of three hours."

I decided that Warwick and Derek should go in first, and we loaded on the boxes. Above the roar of the engines I shouted out last-minute instructions to Warwick before the machine lifted itself off the ground. It whirred upwards, the blast from the blades whipping up the dust, and sidled slowly across the sky towards the mountains sixty miles away. A few minutes later the SA-16 roared down the strip and took off after the helicopter, to watch over it in case of accidents. Donald and I strolled down to the water's edge and sat on a log, looking across the lake. Away down the shore some huskies in their kennels were barking. The only other sound was the water softly lapping against a collec-tion of boats moored just offshore. Behind us, and on one side of the airstrip, stood the weather station. To our right were two or three wooden houses in which the men operat-ing the station lived with their families. A low fringe of cloud stood out in the blue sky and a light wind rustled the reeds. It was very peaceful, and I could not bring myself to believe that in a few hours I might be standing in the white wilderness of the mountains. I settled down to write some duty letters home, while Donald crept about in the reeds and bushes making notes on a variety of birds which abounded here. My letters written, I talked for a while with Henry Coile about Alaskan fishing, then wandered back to the strip and lay down in the sun by our kit.

By 11:30, when I was becoming slightly anxious, some-one heard the SA-16 in the distance and in a few moments it came to rest on the strip. A delighted Colonel Reichert told me that Warwick and Derek, with the kit, had been put down at the junction of the Traleika and Muldrow glaciers, just at the right spot. As we were talking the helicopter came in. Captain Nolan recounted how they had dropped Derek and all the kit at 4,000 feet in Cache Creek, then flown up to the glacier with Warwick on a reconnaissance. All had gone well and Warwick had been set down on an island of stones at the glacier junction. The helicopter had then picked up Derek with some of the kit and flown him up to join Warwick. In the last ferry the remainder of the equipment had been taken up.

It was exciting news; I had an immediate feeling that all would go well on this day. The helicopter was speedily re-fueled and Donald, with 400 pounds of kit, was whirled upwards and away. I sat down with Scott Heater—who had returned with the SA-16—in the shadow of our remaining boxes. He had just started to tell me how rugged the mountains looked, when one of our two ever-attendant photographers—who had also been up in the amphibian—came over and started to speak.

"Say, Mr. Heater, do you think that if the chopper took us in to the glaciers and put us down at the British party's camp, we could follow them for a few days filming? Then perhaps later on we might go in again—I mean we would take our own food and tent, and that."

I was horrified at the idea, but Scotty was more than equal to the situation. He turned on one elbow and looked up at the speaker, fixing him with what I can only describe as a mean look. "Why son, you'd only be a hindrance to these British climbers. They're trained, hardened mountaineers." I did my best to look like one. "They've got years of experience and they've got a job to do, moving on most days. You need special equipment in these mountains, ice axes, ropes, karabiners, pitons, and crampons." He rolled out the words with relish. "You haven't got any of this and you'd need special training. If I had the time I'd put you boys through a course, but it would take too long and in the end you might not measure up.

"Why, if you went out there, these British climbers would have to spend all their time looking after you. Just the glaciers—not even the climbing—are dangerous enough. There are crevasses hundreds of feet deep, just hidden by a thin covering of snow—just waiting for you. You have to probe every step with the axe. For you to go in there would be sudden death. On the glaciers I wouldn't give you boys more than two days to live."

After this speech—a very long one for a strong, silent man—I felt uncertain about going in myself and more than a little apprehensive. The photographer had been visibly affected.

"I guess it would be a kinda tough assignment. Perhaps we could just fly in low and take photographs. Thanks anyway, Mr. Heater. I just thought I'd ask." He drifted disconsolately away to join his companion.

"Scotty," I said, "you've got me scared now. That was a heartening picture you painted."

"Sure," he said, stretching out his long length on the ground. "I had to scare these boys off. They'd just get in your hair." He squinted up into the sun. "But I know the mountains, I'm a mountain man. You see I was born in Idaho at five thousand feet, so I guess I was already half-way there." That set the seal on his judgment.

Over lunch I talked with Captain Nolan, the senior helicopter pilot, about the practical difficulties of picking us up on July 7. He said that if we could make a rendezvous in Cache Creek, at about 4,000 feet, there would be no problem. Difficulties occurred when helicopters of this type were flown above that height. We agreed on the place, and the time as noon.

We wandered back to the strip and saw, in the distance, the small black globe of the helicopter low in the sky. As it slowly set down and the blades ceased to rotate, I felt my nerves tighten. It was now my turn to be projected from the peaceful sunny lake into the mountains. I climbed aboard after loading the kit, feeling as if I were boarding a Hastings for a jump. We clawed our way into the sky and veered sharply off, flying a few hundred feet above tundra. Here and there were large pockets of snow. It looked a sullenly hostile, forbidding landscape, mostly bog and swamp; the thin trees, like great nettles, collapsed against each other, their roots having no hold in the sodden ground. We crossed the McKinley River, shredded by sand bars and ice-sheeted, then up into the foothills, flying through cloud and a light scud of rain. Quite suddenly the cloud cleared and I looked down to see that we were following the stream up into Cache Creek, the mountainsides closing in on the valley. Nolan's voice croaked through on the intercom. "O.K. captain, get ready to jump out with about a hundred pounds of kit; we're dropping you off here."

The wheels touched on the snow-filled stream bed and I

leaped out with my kit and axe and quickly dragged three
boxes after me. The roar of the helicopter died away as I
watched it climb up the valley and disappear over the rim
of hills. It was cold. A chill wind whipped down the valley;
and after the clamor inside the machine everything was
deathly quiet. I looked up the valley at the unbelievable
beauty of the mountains—the white tower of Mount Brooke
soaring into the blue, a cloud trailing from the summit 6,000
feet above me. I took two quick photographs of the scene
and began to build a cairn, which I thought could mark our
future rendezvous. The utter loneliness of these dark lower
hills was quite intimidating. The helicopter seemed to be
taking far too long. I waited, listening for its engine, and
faintly it came, borne by the wind sweeping down from the
snow, growing louder until it filled the whole valley. We
were soon airborne again, climbing until we emerged over
the glacier and I saw the long ridge of Tatum. Before we
landed I was able to take a shot of the two tents below and
the figures standing beside them. Then down to emerge
into the cold of the mountain world. It seemed appropriate
to shake hands with the others and then Warwick and I
were once more whirled off on a short reconnaissance up the
Traleika. We saw very little and it served only to make the
scale of the mountains more difficult to assess. Back at Helicopter Camp, as Warwick had named it, we gave the pilot
a quick nip of whisky and a post card for Bradford Washburn. With "Good luck, and see you in six weeks' time"
from Nolan, the machine rose up and veered away. We
watched it until it was out of sight. We were left in the immense silence of the snows, which was deepened, rather
than disturbed, by the flapping of the tents.

5. The
Glacier: One*

WHEN WE returned to the tents for a meal, cloud barred the
Traleika, denying us a view of our route. The low, slanting
rays of the sun had lost their warmth. Small cold winds scur-
ried across the glacier and chivvied the tents. Derek and I
cooked supper and we enjoyed the last luxury of American
hospitality in the form of the U.S. combat rations which I
had brought up. We were all in high spirits. The whole fly-in
had taken place with a smoothness and a success which had
surpassed all our hopes. Our regard for the Americans had
reached new heights.

The transition from Fairbanks to the mountains in less
than twelve hours had been too sudden. We had not yet
come to terms with our environment. Inside the tents we
could forget the cold intimidation of the ice and the empty
white silence. For Warwick and Derek, who had been first
in, their reactions after crowd had been akin to shock.
"When I had got the kit sorted," Warwick said, "the noise
of the helicopter had died away and the silence was . . .
well, almost crushing. I took a good look at the mountains.
Not a thing moved. I felt sure I was being watched. Once or
twice I jumped round when I thought someone was coming

* See Appendix D.

up behind me. The mountains seemed to be closing in and I was sure I heard voices, but when I looked and listened there was nothing. My own stillness made it worse so I started to walk about and kick stones to make a noise. I can tell you I was pretty glad to hear the helicopter again. I was in a bad state of nerves."

"I felt it as soon as I landed," Derek said. "I kept hearing cars and people walking along pavements. I suppose I wanted to hear them. When Donald came in and we started to get the tents up and our kit out, it all began to seem quite normal and we were less jumpy."

As I lay in my sleeping bag that night I wondered how the Alpine and Himalayan pundits would react to our airborne delivery into the mountains. Was it an ethical method to use? I consoled the purist in me by reasoning that we were merely using aircraft as porters, and by considering the days of relaying and sledging ahead of us and the time saved.

We all slept well that night. In everyone's opinion it was the best sleep since leaving Aldershot. All the worries and the tensions had slackened off and I felt more relaxed than I had for days. Ahead were six weeks of adventure into these unknown mountains—six weeks which could be the best of our lives, in which we would be face to face with the fundamentals of living, with time and weather our only masters. We would learn a great deal about each other and about ourselves as individuals. But above all we would live to the full, striving to gain our objects with all the nerve, skill, and strength we possessed, amid the stark forbidding grandeur and utter beauty of these mountains. We would not leave the mountains quite the same men as those who first flew out of Minchumina.

When breakfast was cooked, Warwick and Donald joined us and we ate it in a tumbled confusion of sleeping bags, pots, stoves, and clothes. We planned to get off that day on the first relay up the glacier. Our three weeks' journey from England had reduced us to a fairly low level of fitness and there had been no march-in to harden us. I planned to bring us back to full fitness by progressively increasing the amount of work done each day. Before the work of loading the sledge and the sorting out of equipment was started, Donald asked for time to make a series of tests to begin his program. We emerged from the tents to be weighed, perform another step test, and have temperatures and pulse rates taken. Surprisingly enough the indexes of the two fittest men had dropped, while those of Donald and myself had improved. Warwick also began his meteorological work, swinging his thermometers and placing other instruments around the camp. The weather was still good. The sun was bright, and harried by a cold gusty wind the clouds moved in and out of the Traleika effectively shutting off the mountains beyond. After lunch we built a cache in which we placed three days' food for the return journey, along with exposed film and other oddments, then packed the sledge with a load of 300 pounds. For this initial journey we decided to have one man out front, route-finding and probing for crevasses, with two pulling. In the rear the fourth man's job was to aid by pushing and act as an anchor and brake when necessary.

The rest of the afternoon was spent idly drinking tea and lazing around waiting for the temperature to drop sufficiently, from the present 30°F, to give us firm, hard snow— a condition essential for the safe crossing of snow bridges and good "glide" for the sledge. At six o'clock we buckled on our sledge harness and were all ready to go. All, that was, except for Donald, who had somehow become inextricably tangled in his harness and innumerable prusik loops. With his long hood down over his face to shut off the cold wind, the slow deliberate movements of his snowshoed feet, and his utter concentration, he gave the impression of an ancient mummer performing some half-forgotten ritual dance. He gyrated slowly before his muffled audience of three, stepping this way and that over the ropes, head down, fumbling with knots and karabiners about his body. He seemed unconscious of our uncouth advice. Donald's performance soon became too much for me and I collapsed into the snow, laughing hysterically. After five minutes of this solitary mime, however, the icy wind removed the humor from the scene and the cries of encouragement and derision changed to threats. Eventually in unhurried solemnity—as if for him time had stood still and the delay had never occurred—he raised his head and said simply, "O.K." We turned with oaths, strained on our traces, and the sledge slid forward.

I felt cautious out in front and conscious of the critical eyes of the others. It was the first time we had worked together as a team in the climbing sense and I knew that each man was weighing up the capabilities and technique of the others. The crevasses occurred often—narrow, but deep; and as the axe broke through the covering of snow the ice fragments tinkled down far into the depths of the glacier. Each time I halted to probe for a suspected crevasse the sledge also stopped and its progress was started again by a combined heave from the two behind me. So we crept on in a series of jerks, the lack of rhythm in our movement making the work more exhausting. After an hour and a half in the lead I handed over to Warwick.

We all moved up one on the harness and I went to the rear. I am no believer in volunteers on expeditions, except for a short passage of particular difficulty when one man's special skill and determination may overcome the problem. When volunteers are relied on, it inevitably means that they do too much. Later in the expedition, on each occasion when someone was allowed to carry on too long, a mishap of some kind occurred, usually as a result of tiredness.

From my rear view the sledge pitched and rolled like a small boat over the waves of ice and snow, its plastic shell twisting and bending with each new stress. It also became apparent that there was no real work for the rear man to do and he could be better employed forward. We continued sledging slowly up the enormous open field of glacier, gradually accustoming ourselves to the small Truger "bear paw" snowshoes which we were wearing. By nine o'clock we had drawn level with a pyramid of stone-covered ice which we had seen from Helicopter Camp. Here we cached the load and after a short rest started back, making a fast return trip with the empty sledge.

Throughout the journey the clouds had lifted only once or twice to reveal the far mountains, and then the veil had closed. These subtle hints at the mysteries beyond tantalized us. Now as we stood outside the tents we saw, far up the glacier, a high, flat-topped peak which seemed to stand at the fork and dominate the whole glacier valley. We continued to watch until the clouds shut it from our view. A name sprang to my mind. "Let's call it Pegasus Peak," I suggested. The others agreed. We had named our first peak.

By mid-afternoon the following day it was freezing hard and we were away up the glacier by three-thirty. Each man carried 40 pounds on his packframe and there was another 400 pounds on the sledge. It was hard going; even with snowshoes we continually broke through the upper crust. Twice in quick succession I fell over, my top-heavy load tilting me forward onto my face, and I was unable to get up without assistance. These falls created humorous diversions in the drudgery of sledging and the others fastened on to the quick laugh easily, Donald accusing me of an ostrich complex.

At the Pyramid Cache we dumped our own loads and pushed on with the sledge. We swung away from the moraine out into the center of the glacier, our movement laborious as antlike we crawled across the white expanse. The crevasses became wider and more cunningly concealed. Twice I went down up to my waist and Derek followed suit once. The experience of suddenly falling was frightening enough, but the looking down between one's jammed snowshoes into the misty blue depths was even more alarming. Most of the trouble was caused by having too little rope between each man so that there was sometimes not enough slack to jump crevasses and the leap was cut short in midair. Or, while poised for a jump, a jerk from the man in front would pull one into a crevasse.

We were becoming more tired; at halts each man stared dully in front of him. There was no conversation. The sledge was heavy and we fought for each yard against the gusty cold wind which whistled eerily through our packframes. The moraine was reached again after six hours and we pitched one tent on a flat space, placing ration boxes inside as ballast. In the small tent we rested a while and drank hot lemonade from a Thermos. Derek fell asleep as we sat there.

Despite our tiredness we returned quickly, and reached the camp at eleven o'clock with the light dimming and the clouds still low—as they had been throughout the journey. Derek and I found the temperature in our tent to be only four degrees above zero but within half an hour, without any form of heating except a lighted candle and the warmth from our bodies, we were able to raise it to 29°F.

The heat of the sun drove us from our sleeping bags the next morning. I felt extremely fit after the fatigue of the previous night and went off happily to the finger-freezing chore of breaking up icicles for the water supply. Even on my return I was still cheerful enough to hurl at the occupants of the other tent such inane parodies of Canadian commercial radio as, "Try Icicle—the new hot-weather drink." I was told—still in the idiom—to "drop dead."

After breakfast we packed the remaining stores on our sledge and packboards, while the wind increased in force, piling up the clouds above the fork of the glacier. Just after one o'clock we saw, far out over the tundra, in the direction of McGonagall Pass, a large four-engined aircraft which we took to be a passing air liner. Fifteen minutes later the same aircraft reappeared much closer overhead. Warwick idly picked up the radio with the vague hope of having a chat with the pilot. To his surprise he received a reply telling him that this was a 74th Air Rescue aircraft making the first three-day check on us. Forgetting his procedure, an amazed Warwick suddenly ejaculated, "Fancy sending such a f——— great bomber." Then, realizing he was still speaking into the set, he hastily apologized. We asked for a weather report and the millibar reading from Minchumina; gave our proposed position in three days' time; made a request for more flares; and, finally, as a typically British ploy, asked for the Test Scores on the next run. We didn't get them. Then the huge plane—it was a Douglas Skymaster—banked away and flew off. We watched in astonished silence until it was lost to sight.

The fact that we were at last moving to a new camp, and the realization that this marked the end of the first stage of our apprenticeship on the glacier, probably accounted for the lightheartedness at lunch time. Too little is known of the conversations and the real behavior of men on expeditions, in spite of the large number of books written about various ventures. Generally the impression given is of a band of stalwart, upright, and very proper Englishmen who, when not keeping a stiff upper lip, occasionally converse politely on a wide variety of subjects, but are never rude to each other or low in thought. Yet I suspect, and even know, that on most modern exploring or climbing expeditions the conversation and behavior of the members was very much like that of our own small party.

When fatigue has dulled the brain and one's mental horizon is bounded by the next meal, or rest, deep, intelligent conversation cannot be expected. Thoughts and conversation turn on the immediate problems of the work in hand, or the weather, or the food. The mind is shallow and amid the hard, slogging drudgery that forms a large part of expedition life, the light relief of humor is doubly appreciated. At rest, at meals, and at any time when there is a chance, humor is snatched at. The humor is not usually subtle; more often it is crude, or rather foolish. Laughs come easily; we would double up in uncontrolled mirth at some remark which in normal life would seem utterly humorless or stupid. Moreover, it is quite inconceivable, and almost unnatural, that a group of people confined together and under nervous strain during weeks of racking toil should remain completely gentlemanly and good-mannered towards each other all the time. So at this meal we prattled inconsequently, enjoying ourselves immensely, and there was much laughter.

"Here's an old grey sock just escaping from camp and I've pinned it down."

"Thanks," said Donald, extending a hand. "It's only been worn once and is far too young to be let out."

Derek, with the air of a connoisseur delicately savoring the bouquet of an old rare brandy, pronounced it, "Exquisite."

Expedition diets seem to produce an excess of gas in the human body. Its expression, uninhibited by normal conventions, threw into gross relief the lavatorial side of our humor.

Occasionally, at any odd time and apropos of nothing, Warwick launched forth into two small ditties, both of which sent Donald into hysterics. One, rendered in a Fred Eccles Goon voice, informed us of the powers of that "wonderful bird the pelican." The other, sung plaintively, ran to only one line. It was simply: "If your aunt had balls she'd be your uncle." As far as I am aware it is the sole example of Hemingway put to music.

We were away at 5:30—this time all in front of the sledge on a longer trace, clipped on with karabiners to a climbing rope. We each carried about forty pounds. Now the first man was protected by the second and the last two were the "huskies." In a short time this method proved itself, and we used it throughout the expedition. In spite of the low temperature and biting wind, the snow was like sand, and at every pause the sledge stuck fast. Sometimes we would all fling our weight forward into the harness four or five times before it would move. Often one man would be on the lip of a crevasse, unable to help for fear of breaking through the overhang, but having the pull transmitted through him. Then suddenly the sledge would be freed, the haulers would lurch forward, and he would be dragged in their wake. If he were lucky he would somehow cross the void. If he did not, there would be a further delay while he was extricated and the whole process would be started again. For the rear man, coping with the forward momentum of those in front and the rearward drag of the sledge, life could be sheer misery; he would often fetch up stretched astride one of the narrower crevasses quite unable to move. Sledging in these conditions is the most temper-straining business I know and often the rear man's fury at the thoughtlessness of his companions would be wonderful to hear.

The Pyramid Cache was reached after two exhausting hours. We changed positions after the halt and I became the

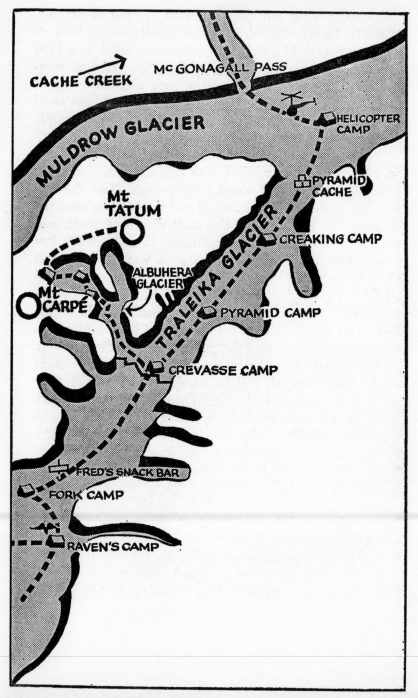

rear man. As we pulled out into the center of the glacier the
sledge overturned several times, imposing annoying delays,
and my temper began to get the better of me. The last straw
came during one of the halts while the leading man
searched for a way across a crevasse. During the pause I
began hauling up the sledge, so that I would have enough
slack in hand to jump another crevasse just in front. I had
almost finished when there was an enormous pull at my
waist and I was jerked unceremoniously off my feet to crash
onto the snow. My companions paused in their flight and
turned to survey my struggles, leaning disinterestedly on
their axes. "Having a lie-down, Jimmy? Feeling tired?"
asked a completely unsympathetic Warwick.

"You bloody idiot, Deacock, why the hell didn't you tell
me you were moving on? How am I expected to cope with a
sledge as well as you three grinning morons? Let's just have
a little thought and cooperation, shall we?"

My appeal met only with jeers. "Poor Uncle Jim's fallen
down. Come on. We're getting cold."

A few minutes later the sledge broke through a snow
bridge and there was another sickening jerk as the shock of
the weight came on me. Luckily, the others took some of
the strain and the sledge was hauled to safety without loss
from the load. The chapter of accidents continued when
Donald's axe broke as he was jumping a crevasse. He was
considerably depressed by this—it was the second he had
broken since our arrival on the glacier. At this point he had
been leading, and now suggested that it was unjustified to
carry on with the sledge without a reconnaissance, in view
of the crevasses. The rest of us were tired and concerned
merely in getting the journey over, so we cried down the
idea. There was a short acrimonious argument and we
pushed on, still with the sledge. Donald took this as a slight
on his judgment as a mountaineer, and withdrew into him-

self. It was a very quiet and rather surly team that just after midnight slogged up the last long haul to the tent on the moraine.

Later, in my sleeping bag, I felt depressed over the quick decline of the party's morale. Perhaps we were a little too critical of each other's skill. The strain of the work and the long hours over crevasses was also putting us on edge. Warwick was a sound leader, but apt to fly into quick tempers, mainly at Derek. Donald was a mixture of sudden *élan* and then complete cautiousness; and Derek had drawn my annoyance more than once with his rather cavalier treatment of safety precautions on the glacier. Yet we had done a good day's work, and there was no doubt that our sledging technique of glacier travel was improving. Perhaps it wasn't such a bad picture after all.

Our sleep was disturbed by rumbling and cracks from the glacier, some of the reverberations sounding like violent thunder just below the tents. We were camped near a large crevasse, and several times when there were loud roars I expected to be shot into its depths by a subsidence of the tortured ice. When we rose we found that a new crack about six inches wide had appeared a couple of feet from one of the tents. We called the place Creaking Camp.

With sixty-pound loads we were off again at seven o'clock pulling a heavy sledge. The snow reminded me of granulated sugar and the sledge built up its own bow wave. A clouded sky hindered our vision and Warwick, who was leading, had a nerve-racking time when we ran into a new maze of enormous crevasses. His tension communicated itself to the rest of us as we watched him probing patiently, yard after yard. When his axe thrusts, meeting no resistance, found a flaw in a bridge he would start back as though from a trap and we could hear the ice chips sounding the the tinkling alarm of danger. It was a trying journey. Each time the crust gave and my foot suddenly dropped a few inches, my heart leaped in alarm. As we steered in towards the moraine the crevasses became larger. The whole glacier creaked and groaned; the reverberations sounded dully, like far-off gunfire, beneath our feet. In the moments of stillness we could hear the snow protesting at the passing of the laden sledge.

Under a large ice pyramid we pitched another tent and made a dump of the stores before returning to Creaking Camp by the same route. This time I led, and in spite of Warwick's route-finding on the outward journey, the way was still a severe test of nerve. Before we reached camp we took Derek forward and he filmed our return.

Except for the very head of the glacier the clouds had cleared and the sun on its low orbit spread fingers of light in the dimmer valley. Above us the peaks were stained pink, and as we gazed up at the ice-fluted ridges and the snow-fields the beauty of their remote splendor stole from our minds the tension of the night's work. We went to sleep soothed with the golden light.

6. The Glacier: Two

DURING THE next two days we moved all the loads from Pyramid Cache and Creaking Camp to establish a new camp under the ice pyramid. It was hard, grinding work, and we were hampered by snowstorms and bad light—so much so that on the first night we could not get through to Pyramid Camp and instead made an intermediate dump on the moraine. The following night, in spite of a top-heavy sledge and bad crevasses, we managed to get as far as the dump in fairly good time. But when we tried to sledge out from the safe shore of the moraine, like a boat going out into a troubled sea, we were forced back again by an intricate pattern of crevasses. No man could put his full weight into the sledge harness for fear that the extra pressure transmitted through his feet would make him break through the tenuous snow bridges. Because of the fixed length of the traces there were times when two or more of us were on snow bridges together. With the additional hazard of the sledge and the loads on our backs, I pessimistically calculated that if two people went down, the other two on top would have little chance of extricating them.

We returned cautiously to the moraine and left the sledge. Then with light loads, including a tent, we traced a route through to Pyramid Camp, marking it with flags. At the pyramid we erected a second tent, placing flattened-out cartons between the ice and the floor cloth. This extra insulation was necessary, for both Donald's and Warwick's air mattresses had slow punctures and complete repair was not possible.

We returned to the dump along the moraine and lashed to our packboards loads of at least eighty pounds. The moraine was cut by enormous crevasses, most of which were open, but not a few were negotiable by impressive snow bridges. It was a testing course led admirably by Warwick. On some of the snow bridges we tiptoed as lightly as the heavy loads would allow; on others we crawled, trying to spread the weight as much as possible, hoping the belays were good ones. Jumping crevasses with an eighty-pound load is not a recommended pastime. If we were lucky the takeoffs were good, but once launched across the void each man could feel the load dragging him down into the icicle-toothed depths. On several, I made trial run-ups to the brink before a final desperate leap. In this game the shorter Derek was at a tremendous disadvantage, but by sheer bounce he managed to fling himself across each one. By far the worst were the jumps that were up as well as across. On several occasions only one foot would reach the other side, but we developed a technique to overcome this last fatal gravity pull. As the jumper was about to land, the man already across would, at the crucial moment, give the rope a sharp tug, impelling the airborne unfortunate forward those few vital extra inches to gain the other side. The landing under the crushing weight was a hazard in itself; the risk of a sprained or broken ankle was considerable.

The crevasse-hopping game, we thought, was not worth a candle, and our return journey to the dump was made by the glacier. As we went we improved our previous route into a possible one for the sledge. This we used for the final drag up to Pyramid Camp, a journey made nightmarish by the awful subterranean rumblings of the glacier. At each step we expected to be involved in a minor earthquake. Donald uncharacteristically went down twice, though not very far. Near the end of the journey, when he and I were both crossing a large snow bridge, the whole surface suddenly dropped several inches. We remained for a few trancelike moments rooted to the spot, our stomachs floating somewhat higher than normal. The spell broken, our strangely high-pitched shouts drove the others forward and we were dragged clear of the danger spot.

After eleven hours of lively work, at eight that morning we pulled the last load up onto the moraine. We were too tired to unpack the sledge. A rest and a supper of pemmican hoosh helped us appreciate the view which this camp gave us. The sky was clear and opalescent. Far beyond the sentinel of Pegasus Peak we could see some of the glistening peaks which enclosed the head of the glacier like a wall. Distantly came the boom and crash of innumerable, unseen avalanches.

The sun bore down on us, filling the tent with heavy airless heat, and we slept fitfully. In the late afternoon the throb of aircraft engines broke in upon us and we scrambled, bemused with sleep, out onto the moraine. Warwick and Donald acted as watchers while Derek lit a flare and then stood by with his camera. The orange smoke of the flare trailed through the camp. I spoke into the set. "Hello, British mountaineering party calling. We are almost level with ice fall from Tatum and Carpe and have lit a flare."

A pause, then from the aircraft flying high overhead, "O.K. We've got you. We're coming down for a drop."

We watched as the SA-16 flew on up the glacier, losing height rapidly until it appeared to be flying into the mountain wall enclosing the head. It seemed an age before it turned, and for the first time we realized the vastness of our surroundings. The plane, now only a tiny symbol against the vast snows, made a large slow circle, still losing height. Yet so enormous was the cirque that even this spacious maneuver appeared as no more than a small gyration in the mountain arena. After one trial run some thousand feet above the glacier, the amphibian returned to the cirque and spiraled down even lower. Like a roaring, rushing bird it came at us, less than 200 feet up. As it swept over the camp two tiny packages on streamers left the door and fell a few yards away. It was a superb exhibition of skill.

"Oh first class . . . just the job. We've got them."

"Right. Can you give us your position in three days' time?"

"Yes, we'll be right opposite the ice fall. Could you give a drop of two ice axes? We've broken our spare."

"O.K. Will do. Will you risk a mail drop?"

"Yes, we certainly will. Could we have a time check now?"

"It's just seventeen hundred hours. If that's all, we're off. Good luck—be seeing you."

"Goodbye and thanks for a wonderful drop."

The aircraft was soon out of sight and we examined the "wonderful drop." It was just some more flares.

No one could sleep after the excitement of the drop so we made an early breakfast.

At nine-thirty we were ready to start away in the bright evening sunlight. After the experiences of the day before we decided to make a reconnaissance for a sledge route, going ahead on foot with light loads. In two hours of fast moving, over good snow and ice, I led through almost to the end of the moraine. Here, where the pressure was greatest, near the fork of the glacier and opposite the ice fall, the surface had been forced up and riven by crevasses into a creak-

ing, disintegrating wasteland of rock-covered ice slag
heaps. We decided to look for a campsite which we could
occupy for several days, rather than venture out into the
center of the glacier with its hidden horrors. After an hour
of searching we found a level site and put up our old green
Meade tent. We were encircled by large crevasses; our small
island was accessible only by means of a jump over a nasty
green and black pit. But the site was at least level and
slightly sheltered. We had a hot drink from the Thermos
and while we chewed chocolate and biscuits we traced a
route up to the col between Tatum and Carpe. It lay up a
glacier tributary which tumbled in an ice fall, to meet the
Traleika, two miles away from our campsite.

On the way back an almost perfect sledge route was confirmed by Donald. It was a virtual roadway of smooth snow
and ice which seemed to carry on past Crevasse Camp—as
we now called it—for some distance up the glacier. We carefully marked it with route flags, determined that whatever
happened we would occupy Crevasse Camp the next night.
By four-thirty we were back in camp, and an hour later had
finished our pemmican supper. The night's work had been a
satisfying one, for we had established a temporary base
camp from which we would make our first attempts on the
virgin peaks. Derek, who had suffered from increasing tiredness for the past four days, was morose and irritable. I had
noticed his quick, sensitive reaction to some of Warwick's
barbed remarks, and Warwick seemed to delight in the effect of his attacks. The bad feeling between them stemmed
from the fact that Warwick had never forgiven Derek for
damaging his car in London, just before we left. At the time,
Derek had protested his innocence and refused to make
good the damage. Now, magnified under the strain of hard
and dangerous work, the old annoyance rankled in War-

wick's mind and he sought relief from his own bad temper, and consolation for the injury in the past, by sinking the fangs of his discontent into Derek.

As we sat outside the tents enjoying the early warmth of the sun's rays and drinking our last cups of tea, Warwick looked at the silent Derek mischievously, and taunted, "Why don't you cheer up, you miserable monster?"

"I'm just browned off. I always am when I'm as tired as this." Derek did not look up, but continued to look intently and miserably into his mug of tea.

His victim nettled, Warwick jeered, "That's a bloody lot of good in the mountains."

Derek rose suddenly; the tea from the mug, still in his hand, slopped over, staining the snow and splashing Warwick's boots. His other fist was clenched hard and his tired, sweat-streaked face was alive with anger. There was complete silence as they faced each other, Derek trembling with rage and Warwick looking surprised, almost bewildered. I moved forward on my seat ready to prevent the fight which appeared imminent. There was a crash as Derek's mug, flung with vicious force, hit the rocks at Warwick's feet and bounced into the snow spraying a spume of tea. Then with venomous intensity he shouted, "For Christ's sake leave me alone, you bastard." The words were spat hatefully in Warwick's upturned face.

Warwick, shaken by the violence and hate he had aroused, appealed to Donald and myself: ". . . and I've got to live with this."

Derek slouched away to his tent which he unfortunately shared with Warwick.

I said, "He's going to hit you soon, Warwick, and it's obvious that it would be fatal for the expedition. Why go on antagonizing him? Why not forget the business in London?

With only four of us, always roped together wherever we go, there's no escape from one another. Derek's probably going to be next to you on the rope tomorrow and you are going to depend on him." I made a resolution to change over the tent occupants when we arrived in Crevasse Camp.

7. *Rest Day*

By CUTTING out all possible delays and driving ourselves hard for nine hours, we made two ferries from Pyramid Camp to Crevasse Camp. We were finally home and dry by six o'clock in the morning of June 4. After eight days of grinding work we planned to have a break, for two days, to establish the camp and rest ourselves before starting on the first climb. We were up again, just after midday, in order to get back to normal routine and go to bed at night for a change. While Warwick and Derek constructed tent platforms and generally made the camp more comfortable, Donald and I ventured out into the center of the glacier. On a level spot, opposite the camp, we marked out a dropping zone about the size of a football pitch. Here we would take the vital drop of axes and mail on the following day. The exciting thought of mail infected us all and brought up the controversial subject of whether the air support was more nuisance than it was worth.

Warwick was dead against it on account of loss of sleep. His point was valid; we had already lost several hours of rest because of the aircraft's arrival during the day. But I felt I couldn't ask the U.S.A.F. to fly over at night, which was our working time. Nonetheless, mail was a valuable morale factor and as we had to have this air rescue cover there was not much we could do about it. By far my greatest worry, as leader, was that first one flight and then another

73

would fail to locate us. This might start off a full-scale rescue operation which, besides being unnecessary, was certain to receive publicity and cause relatives pointless worry.

The rest of the day passed quickly. The sun, coming through the clouds, took its toll of the snow bridges all all around us and we could hear torrents of water running through the crevasses. That night we slept well despite the creaking of the glacier, and rose at the more normal time of eight o'clock. We spent most of the day feeding up on large meals and preparing our kit for the climb. Donald and I sorted rations while the others cooked a large, heavy cake in an improvised oven. It was a scene of peaceful domesticity as we pottered around amiably among the slag heaps. The place seemed to have been our home for weeks. In the evening we all crawled into one tent to eat a large curried stew, then tinned strawberries from our luxuries box, followed by the sweet—but leaden—cake. After coffee and a hot whisky toddy we tottered off, feeling bloated, to the enfolding warmth of our sleeping bags.

The aircraft caught us, still asleep, just after eight o'clock, and we went befuddled to our various tasks. The drop-zone party of Donald and Warwick set out, a zombielike Deacock stumbling along swearing violently at all aircraft. He was dressed in his red windproofs to act as a marker for the drop. I wondered what his reactions would be if, with their usual accuracy, the 74th squadron registered a direct hit with a pair of axes. The aircraft, the figures on the glacier, and the falling parachute bearing the axes made a dramatic picture which Derek attempted to record on film from the top of a slag-covered *sérac*.

While Donald cooked breakfast we settled down to the very private pleasure of our letters. I had six from Jeanne, and it seemed quite incongruous to be reading of happenings in Germany and at home, sitting 8,000 miles away on an Alaskan glacier. Warwick's fiancée had included a plush box of Fortnum and Mason's crystallized fruits. It was very welcome, of course, but I feel that this loving gesture sealed irrevocably his bachelor fate, for he was married five months after we returned to England.

In the afternoon loads were set out and we took our pick, each man hoping to get the lightest one. The weighing machine was the final arbiter, and this time they were all within a pound or two of fifty-five pounds, but no one likes to think that he is carrying a heavier load than the next man on an exacting journey. Ideally, everyone should carry the same load; then there are few excuses in which the weary can indulge.

The ice fall was big, well over a mile in length and with a total fall of about two thousand feet. It was comparable in size to the one which flows from the Western Cwm on Everest, but lacking its difficulty, for it was possible to escape the worst areas by a traverse along its left bank. All day I had watched for avalanches from a hanging glacier above to sweep across our path. But none came. It was obvious, however, that we must move extremely fast across the long traverse, which was threatened throughout its entire length. Possibly the letters from home caused my mood of introspection. I felt a sense of foreboding about that night's climb up the long ice fall. It was not really fear, but rather the keying up of mind and body as before a race. Intermingled with these thoughts was a feeling of anxiety for the safety of the other three. I felt utterly responsible for their lives and for the unhappiness which a tragedy would bring to their families. The thought of my own wife—alone in England writing the letters which had arrived by air only that day—made me feel irresponsible and selfish for undertaking this whole business.

The supper took a long time to cook—the stove was giving

Warwick a great deal of trouble. To while away the time he
produced from the bottom of his kit bag a remarkable magazine called *Sexology,* which he had been given by the re-
ceptionist at Murphy Hall ("I guess this might help to pass
those long evenings"). As the magazine's correspondence
columns showed, its readers suffered from an astonishing
variety of acutely personal problems which gave us considerable amusement. There was a letter from an Alaskan
reader which almost prompted us to compose a request for
advice on behalf of Warwick—who often confessed, on his
daily activity and food-consumption form, to being troubled
by thoughts of Marilyn Monroe. We found this evidence of
undoubted virility rather bizarre and enviable in these frigid
wastes. In the end the magazine was presented to Donald,
for we felt that as a document it was of medical importance.

After supper, and just before midnight, we swung on our
packs and roped up for the journey to the foot of the ice fall.

8. The Ascent
to Waggoner's Col

OUR LATE START was unfortunate, but even more unfortunate was my exit from the camp. In the first few yards I slipped on a slight incline and shot through the snow covering of a crevasse I was probing, to be mercifully held at chest depth by Donald. The crevasse having thus been well marked for them, the others had no difficulty in negotiating it. We carried on across the glacier, slowly and cautiously, to the *séracs* which marked its fringe. Here Donald took over and threaded us through a tortuous tangle of *sérac* and crevasse with many a Gaelic version of the snowshoe shuffle over the trickier parts. The *séracs* debouched onto a long snow slope which led up to the bergschrund.

At the foot of the slope we paused for a rest and watched while the crimson glory of the sunset, staining the sky above McGonagall Pass, was slowly vanquished by the more delicate shades of the sunrise spreading its fresh light across the sky. In the hour preceding this changeover the light was at its worst. On the glacier it made crevasse-finding infinitely more difficult, and in this grey hour the morale of the party always slumped. It was in this period that things went wrong and tempers flared.

We started up the steep hard snow. On the lip of the bergschrund we divided into two ropes. The bergschrund—a

77

great gulf splitting the glacier away from its confining walls —was crossed easily in a long traverse over a bridge of hard avalanche debris. It marked the tip of a long menacing finger of avalanche which pointed down from the hanging glacier above. We plodded up the rubble, sinking to our knees with every step. It was desperately tiring but speed was essential, and we paused only to wipe the sweat from our eyes and search the menacing ice blocks above us for signs of movement. We traversed left across a long snow ramp, enjoying the respite from the upwards grind, before continuing diagonally, but still climbing, to the point where a long rock rib barred our way.

Warwick and I judged it safer to try and cross it lower down, but the others, unwilling to lose the height, continued on their previous line. We moved carefully, belaying each other up the short pitches. The rock was shattered and rotten to the touch; no hold was safe. We climbed hopefully, our passage marked by loosened fragments cartwheeling and twisting in the air on their downward plunge to the bergschrund. It was not good for the nerves or balance to dwell on the long, floating parabola of their flight.

Beyond the rib we rested momentarily in more avalanche debris and waited for Derek and Donald. They soon joined us, Donald bleeding from a long cut on the bridge of his nose, sustained, he ruefully told us, in a twenty-foot fall higher up on the rib. A long slope of hummocked avalanche snow followed, which brought us up against another rib, this time of steep ice. We were now past the beginning of the ice fall but high above it and in the center of the menaced area. Having donned crampons we steadily mounted the flank of the rib. At the top we could see that our way lay across an ice slope which plunged steeply down into the ice fall. The height we had gained had enabled us to avoid the worst part of the fall, and a traverse of the slope would bring us into its more passable upper reaches.

Warwick and I led out onto the traverse. It was not steep at the beginning, and we were able to move together. After a few steps we were confronted by a fissure in the ice, per- haps five feet wide. The edge on our side was a foot or more lower than the far one, and the ice beyond became much steeper. Warwick moved back a few paces to give himself a run-up for the jump. The landing on the sloping ice of the far side was difficult and dangerous. I belayed him, made sure there was enough slack, and then he pounded forward as fast as his fifty-five-pound load would allow. Taking a pack off seemed a waste of time, and by now we were prac- tised crevasse-jumpers. He took off with a powerful lunge and landed with plenty to spare, his crampons punching in deeply with the force of his weight and his load. He swayed off balance. I checked him with the rope. One small step, and he had recovered. I watched while he cut a small platform on which to base himself while he belayed me. The boots I was wearing were the Himalayan type, padded and cum- bersome, with large canvas outer covers. They fitted well but did not give good support, and I seemed to be divorced from my crampons. I was not confident of my climbing abil- ity in them and was apprehensive about the landing on the far side.

"Right," said Warwick.

I stumbled forward in a run, my axe held out in front. As I slammed my foot down for the takeoff it twisted under me and I fell, rather than leaped, forward. I landed with my stomach across the far edge, winding myself, my feet kicking into space below. Instinctively I had driven the axe pick in; this and the taut rope held me. My right crampon caught a projection below. I levered myself forward. With a

crack the hold broke. My body dropped. The upward pull
as my arm came up levered the axe out. I dangled chest-
deep, my weight full on the rope.

"Christ, Jimmy!" Warwick was alarmed. "Steady, don't
do that again. This stance isn't all that bloody good."

I felt even more insecure. By twisting one foot I was able
to get two crampon points into the crevasse wall and lever
myself up a few inches. It was enough. Overarm I drove the
axe in again and pulled myself up.

"Hold me while I have another bash."

The axe went in with a solid, satisfying noise. I hauled
again, dragged my stomach over, and floundered forward
on my knees.

"Sorry, Warwick, it's these blasted boots." It sounded like
a lame excuse for my own failing.

"Yes, but watch it next time," Warwick said shortly.

I was still rather shaky, and my confidence in my performance in this present footwear had suffered. There was
only one way to regain it. "Look, we can lead through on
this and I'll start," I said.

"O.K., but take it easy." Warwick looked dubious. The
incident and my excuse had obviously shaken his trust in
me. I felt apprehensive and depressed. This was no place for
lack of confidence between us.

"Have you got me?" He nodded and I moved out on the
traverse. I advanced steadily across the ice, cutting a chain
of small steps with quick, rhythmic blows. Standing upright, well out from the slope, based on twenty steel points,
balancing the pull of the load against the swing and shock
of the axe as it cut in, I felt my confidence begin to return as
I progressed. The ice particles slithered and bounced down
the slope. Five or six blows, then a step. The rear foot is
brought forward, is placed carefully, unhurriedly; the crampon points sink in; the body weight shifts; the axe swings

again. My pack was part of me. I felt compact and capable. The rope looped and pulled behind me as I moved steadily from one small incut platform to the next. I became increasingly conscious of being the only upright thing in a world of slanting lines and angled ice.

Engrossed in the work and feeling the delight of my returned confidence, I had come almost to the end of the rope when shouts from Warwick arrested me. I cut a platform, drove in a piton to which I attached myself, then took the rope round my waist and called him on. He came across deliberately and steadily. I saw the other pair begin their traverse. Warwick passed and began cutting. Rope length after rope length we moved across the face and finally arrived in the snowy upper section of the ice fall. Here we waited for the others. Before moving off again we all tied onto one rope for added security. Warwick led off into the forest of *séracs* and soft-mouthed chasms.

Below us, in the lower ice fall, the snow was melting and collapsing into the crevasses, the heavy falls booming hollowly in the still air. The sun glared down out of a clear sky, searing into the piled blocks of ice which hung over us, menacing and silent. At any moment the heat might free them from their frozen immobility. Our ears were alert for any warning sound, but there would be no escape from an ice avalanche.

For nine hours we had been moving with scarcely a halt. Two more hours, perhaps, would see us out of the threatened area. Around tottering *séracs* and over delicate, softening, snow bridges we wound our way, never moving more than one at a time, from one belay to the next. We were all tired. The race against the sun, with heavy loads on our first climb, had drained our strength. Yet still the utmost concentration was needed. Each man depended implicitly upon the others for his safety, and a moment's carelessness or indifference

might endanger the whole party. It was a fine lead by Warwick, requiring nerve and patience, and slowly in his train
he drew our caterpillar length through this dangerous,
threatened area onto the smoother, safer slopes beyond.

We moved left, into the bowl formed by the upper glacier,
and headed towards the face which lead up to the col. Into
this bowl, with its gleaming white floor and sides, the sun
poured its brilliant light. From every side the glare was
reflected in blinding, stabbing rays and stifling heat. Across
this airless, dazzling suntrap, in snow that was like sand,
we plodded with slow, dead steps. Each man bowed, head
down, in his own mute, dull world of fatigue, conscious only
of the heat, the brilliant light, and the numbing drag of his
pack. There was no joy in the mountains.

Sweat-drenched, I forced one foot in front of the other,
slipping occasionally and being jerked by Warwick in front
—which irritated me—and sometimes being tugged from
behind by one of the others, which annoyed me even more.
I was too tired to voice my feelings. Our goal was a patch of
stones in the center of the glacial bowl and slowly we
dragged ourselves towards them. We took so long to get
there that at times I thought they were a mirage, but finally
at eleven o'clock we arrived and halted. I sank down beside
Warwick and leaned back against my pack. The relief was
enormous. Donald and Derek came up and slumped down.
I took off my goggles and squinted at Warwick and the
others. Their cream-daubed faces were sweat-stained and
utterly weary. The col was still eight hundred feet above
us. I wondered if we would ever get there.

We brewed lemonade over a hexamine-tablet fire and
silently ate biscuits and chocolate. The food felt like mud in
my mouth, but the lemonade was like nectar. After an hour
we reluctantly heaved on our packs and Warwick immediately moved off in the lead. I had meant to change the

lead to the other pair, but had forgotten. There was no good axe belay and Warwick was already probing some yards ahead. Some protection was necessary, and I took the rope round my body in a standing belay. By this time he was almost at the full extent of the rope and had stopped, probing carefully. For a moment he ceased his investigation and turned his head to call over one shoulder, "I think I'm on a snow bridge."

I braced myself; the others—interested spectators—had not moved. He made another thrust with his axe and then abruptly and in complete silence he dropped from view. I had the impression of his body, bolt upright, going down as I imagined an executed man falls through a trap door. The rope began to run out across my shoulders. I felt the heat of its friction. I began to check it, but as it slowed, the pull became too much and I was impelled forward, in a few staggering steps, until jerked, face downwards, into the snow. By now I had stopped the runout but was towed forward by the weight of Warwick's falling body, towards the hole. I dug in my elbows and showshoes, forcing my body into the snow, trying desperately to stop myself. Through my brain two thoughts hammered. *I must stay on top or he's done for. If he dies the expedition's finished.*

My ploughlike progress began to slow. I felt the pull from behind and stopped. Then the strain came fully upon my right arm, with which I was holding Warwick. I thought it was coming out of its socket. I could not hold the rope much longer. Twisting slightly, with my other hand I managed to unclip the rope from the waist karabiner. I yelled for Donald to take in the slack and anchor the rope and Warwick. The strain came off and I staggered to my feet, then with my own axe anchored the rope through a loop. I crawled forward to the hole and was surprised to find that it was so large. There was a large overhang to the crevasse from which long, thick, pointed icicles hung. I looked down into the misty blueness and called, "Warwick, are you all right?"

There was silence. I could see nothing of him; the light did not penetrate far, and I could see down only about twenty or thirty feet. An awful doubt seeped into my mind. Was he unconscious or dead? A picture of his crumpled body imprinted itself on my brain. The full horror, and the knowledge of its effect on the others and the expedition, filled me with a rising fear. At least the rope had not broken or gone slack—he must be hanging. I shouted again, louder this time, and from below—a long way off—Warwick's voice came to me weakly and thinly out of the blue-black vault.

"I'm all right, I think. How are the others?"

"Everyone's O.K. We'll have you out in a moment. We'll use the double-rope method."

"Can you lower me slightly, so that I can get down to a ledge, which I can just touch, then I'll pass up my kit."

His voice was stronger now and there was a note of controlled resolution in it which heartened me. He asked, "Shall I put crampons on?"

"Yes," I shouted, "we'll lower you and send a rope down for your kit." I crawled back to the others who waited expectantly. Their faces had thrown off the fatigue.

"He's all right. We'll use the stirrup method to raise him. Slacken off your rope a little, so that he can reach a ledge, Donald." I crawled back with a rope, knotted a loop in one end and lowered it. It ran out a good fifty feet before Warwick caught it. I hauled up the heavy packboard but near the top a snowshoe came off and fell, striking Warwick on the head. His agonized and shocked cry sounded almost pitiful coming from the depths. The rope was lowered again. He already had one foot in a loop on the climbing rope, taking the strain off his chest, and into the second he put his other foot. Under the rope, near the edge, I placed an axe to act as a roller. I stayed near the lip calling out, "Left, right, left, right," to coordinate his efforts with those of Derek and Donald on the other ends of the ropes.

Inch by inch each rope slid through the snow. I groveled with my bare hands, trying to keep the ropes from cutting too deeply into the overhang, or entwining one with the other. In a short while my fingers had turned deadly white and my hands were streaked with blood where the skin had been stripped by the abrasive snow. They became quite useless. Derek, wearing gloves, took over from me and there was a brief pause while I brought some life back into my hands. Then the struggle began again. Left, right; haul in a foot; a quick turn around the axe and secure. The rope stretched like elastic with the strain, losing precious inches of height gained. There was nothing—no heat, no mountains, no fatigue—only the rope creeping slowly forward through the snow and the agonizing effort and stress of keeping the inches gained.

Inch by inch we raised him, hoping that he could fight off the cold and shock, and retain enough strength to help himself. Then Derek lowered a loop and in a moment Warwick's face appeared above the snow. He looked grey and exhausted. He gave a crooked grin and said "Hulloo" in a Fred Eccles Goon voice before he was hauled over the edge. Derek supported him as he walked forward and an enormous relief took the tautness from me. I felt drained and tired. Donald pushed a thermometer into Warwick's mouth (for the cause of science, it registered 95.8°F) and diagnosed shock. We put Warwick into his sleeping bag and, at Donald's suggestion, put up the tent on the island of stones to camp there until that night.

While we ate supper Warwick told this story. "I didn't feel the bridge go. There was that feeling you get parachuting from a balloon, when your stomach floats upwards and in its place there's only an empty breathlessness. I felt myself spinning and bouncing against the walls: I wasn't particularly worried. All I could think was 'feet and knees together and the best of luck.' Then I stopped. There was no jerk—just a lot of yo-yoing about. I thought, 'Jim's held me.' Somehow I'd turned upside-down. I hadn't realized it until I saw my right leg caught up by the rope above my head. It came free easily and I swung down and found I was just above a small ledge. Had I not been held I'd have hit it. Underneath, the crevasse was just a large black hole. I knew I'd been lucky, but I wasn't particularly scared—the shock hadn't come yet. I only felt very lonely and in spite of the rope holding me I suddenly felt that something must have happened to you three. Then I heard Jimmy's voice. Christ, I was glad. I could just see your head against the sky, so I knew I wasn't hearing things. It was a good thing we practiced this crevasse rescue technique on the ship. Another five minutes and I'd have been helpless. The cold got right into me. I was utterly shagged and when I got to the top I felt like crying. Then Donald, you monster, rammed that bloody thermometer in my mouth. I knew I'd been rescued then."

We had raised him in twenty minutes. There was no doubt that the previous crevasse rescue practice; the technique of the chest harness, which had probably saved him from a broken back; the Tarbuck knot; and quick action had helped to save his life.

We lay down in our sleeping bags, crammed into the tiny tent. After the others were asleep I remained awake thinking about the accident. I felt guilty about my lack of thought over protecting Warwick. Had I gone forward a few yards I could have made a good safe axe belay and he would only have gone down a foot or two. It was my fault that the whole thing had been so serious. But then he shouldn't have started off so suddenly without warning. He had been too long in the lead and was too tired. My mistake was in not having asked someone else to lead. The earlier feelings of inadequacy rose again in me.

Outside, a small avalanche from the nearby cliffs rattled a few stones lightly against the tent. Still asleep, Warwick curved a protective arm around his head and cried out, in a frightened, quavering whimper, then was quiet. I felt a great pity for him. What effect would this accident have on his nerves, coming only six months after his hundred-foot fall in Wales? We would all need a good deal of nerve in the weeks to come.

Our start early the next morning was delayed by an hour or more of fishing in the crevasse for the missing snowshoe, using an ice axe as a hook. It was eventually brought to the surface. By the time we had ascended, in vile snow, to the bergschrund we were all exhausted. What lay beyond was even worse. The long grind, up the fifty-degree, rock-covered ice slope to the col, will remain in my mind as one of my most agonizing climbs. We zigzagged up with slow steps, Donald in front forcing the pace. It was far too fast, and in our tiredness we cursed and swore at each other, and mostly at Donald, for the tugging and jerking on the rope. Donald went faster. I later learned that he did this when near the end of his strength, driving himself as hard as possible as though racing against the ebbing of his energy. It seemed quite stupid, for he ran the risk of losing this race and wrecking himself, imposing an exhausted man on the party. We reached the top at the limit of our strength and collapsed on the rock and into the snow.

One by one we staggered to our feet and went to see what lay beyond the col. We looked out across the white roadway of the Muldrow Glacier below, out of our world of snow, ice, and rock, into the misty greens and blues of the tundra. To

our right, and behind us, rose the meringuelike slope of
Carpé. The long ridge of Tatum climbed into the blue to
the north. Lying back, above the head of the Muldrow, we
could just make out the outline of McKinley's summit, which
wore lightly a misty halo of feathery cloud.

When we had recovered sufficiently, we began to construct
a rock platform for the tent. Derek, for an artist, had a fine
practical sense and he directed operations for building the
platform out from the steep slope. For the floor he split
off flat sections of slatelike rock, using a piton hammer and
a piton as a chisel. In our parlous state Donald and I found
it exhausting, tedious work while Warwick, too faint and
weak to help, lay on a small ledge of rock above.

When the platform was finished we put up the small
orange tent. It stood jutting out from the steep slope. While
the others rested I cooked a meal, and by two o'clock in the
afternoon we were all down on our sleeping bags. Donald
and I tried unsuccessfully to get to sleep in the stifling
heat of the tent. Outside, the other two occupied the only
other level place on the small rock ledge above. An hour later
the great C-54 was over, the closing mist making it difficult
for us to see it. Warwick spoke on the wireless, received a
time check, and gave our position back on the glacier in
72 hours' time. No one slept again, and at six I cooked the
supper. When we did pile into the tent we slept head to
toe, and Derek, the last man in, did not touch the floor all
night. I had drawn the outside berth and lay as in a ham-
mock held by the thin walls of the tent which bulged out
over five hundred feet of space. At least it was softer than
the stones, and the stitching was good.

Slowly I became aware of the pain creeping up my legs.
I awoke with a start with the cramp knotting and tightening
my muscles from ankle to thigh, like twisted bands of elastic
under strain. The agony was frightful and I tried to get up,

panicking for fear a tendon would give. I was pinned by the weight of the others, and Donald lay across my legs. I could not move.

"Donald, Donald," I whispered, my throat tight and restricted with the effort of suppressing the rising pain. There was no reply. I could feel the sweat beads standing out cold on my face.

"For goodness' sake move, Donald. This cramp's killing."

The gentle sleepy voice came muffled from his sleeping bag.

"Och, sorry."

He rolled over slightly and I was able to move my legs a little inside my bag, but the pain still gripped them.

"What can I do to stop it?" I asked anxiously.

"Oh nothing. It'll pass off," said Donald sleepily and soothingly. Having taken my plight to his professional heart he fell asleep.

Cursing, I wriggled my imprisoned legs as best I could and the pain slowly subsided, releasing the tension from my muscles. I lay back on my unwaking companions.

9. Tatum

THE ALARM shrilled at one-thirty and while I brewed water by the door the others crouched, huddled together in their sleeping bags at the far end of the tent. To save time Donald introduced us to "brose." Each man's mug was half-filled with dry porage, lumps of chocolate, and raisins, and boiling water was added. Then a vigorous stirring and when the water was absorbed, breakfast was ready. We found it delicious and filling. There is the added advantage that one billy of water suffices for the whole breakfast—tea and brose.

At three-thirty Donald and Warwick left, followed by Derek and me a few minutes later. Climbing on two ropes is normally faster than moving four together, and Derek and I could also film the others. The making of a film was an integral part of our program, and we gave it equal priority with the other "secondary" objects of the expedition.

Many climbers object to cine filming because it diverts effort from the main aim. This objection is a valid one; the taking of a good film, one that is an artistic and technical success as well as a true record, requires a great deal of extra effort and time. Moving in two parties, as we did on Tatum, obviates many of the difficulties. When the climbers move together, the photographer's demands can seriously affect the party's progress and work.

I believe, however, that the traveler still has a duty to

tell of what he has done and seen. Books and lectures were once his only medium, but with the film, and perhaps more so with television, the means of communicating with a wider public has become largely visual. This is not an entirely new factor, but the interest and appeal of travelers' tales told by film grows rapidly. Yet the film of high quality of a mountaineering expedition, which catches not only the atmosphere but the spirit of the enterprise, has not been made. We hoped to prove that this could be done by ama-teurs with light equipment, and in such a way that it did not interfere with the main work of the expedition.

We moved along the broad ridge keeping well to the right, away from the enormous cornices which overhung the Muldrow side. The snow was hard, and we climbed steadily towards the base of a rock step. We took a line up its right flank, climbing carefully up the steep, shattered rock to emerge again on the snow ridge, now much narrower. The sky was filled with large, ponderous clouds tinged by a pale blue light. The air was still. Our frosted breath dissolved quickly. The snow was softer now, and we followed the deep tracks of the others, the angle just steep enough to call for effort. As we approached a minor summit on the ridge, it splayed out into a wide expanse, and we traversed across a steep slope to arrive on an airy knife-edge of hard snow which led down to a large plateau. The sides fell away sheerly and we belayed each other carefully as we tight-roped along the spine of snow. It was perhaps only fifty yards—merely a fragment of the ascent—but I felt, as I moved in space, high above the world along this line of snow which communed with the sky, a feeling of utter remoteness. This, allied with the test of nerve, balance, and skill, pro-duced an exultant feeling of physical well-being which seemed to be communicated by the rope between us. I felt vibrantly alive and attuned to all the joy, the mystery, and the challenge of the mountains. With new vigor we ploughed our way across the deep snow of the plateau to join the others who were resting.

Warwick produced his Thermos and we sat together in the snow and sipped hot tea. With his glasses Donald scanned the Muldrow, thousands of feet below us, its upper reaches cloud-swathed. He suddenly grabbed Warwick's arm and said, "I can see the Americans."

"Here, let me have a shufti," urged Warwick. He grabbed the glasses and after a moment said, "Yes, they're just coming into camp." He passed the binoculars to me.

Through the glasses I could see two black triangles of tents and four dots moving down a track in the snow. At the tents they stopped and disappeared inside. Up the glacier their track was visible winding in and out of the crevasses. We viewed the marks of their efforts as the gods must see them. Men, tiny forked creatures, who for a moment crawl antlike across these vast uplifted snows and then are gone, wind and blizzard wiping out the traces of their presence, leaving, perhaps, as the only reminder of their passing, a rusting, jagged, empty food tin half-buried in the snow.

To our right, about fifty yards away, the ridge narrowed to a serrated blade which cut steeply into the sky, the side visible to us falling in one sheer, shining sweep of ice a thousand feet or more to the hanging glacier. The others set off, and we watched and photographed them as Donald led out onto the ridge. It was too narrow to walk upon, so Donald, belayed by Warwick and holding the ridge-top with one hand, cut steps along its flank just below the crest. Warwick led through and then Donald. By now they were about a third of the way along the ridge with Warwick sitting *à cheval* while he protected Donald.

We moved up to the ridge and found the ice to be of a granulated type in which steps soon crumbled. To arrest

this deterioration, and thus to speed our return, Derek and
I improved on the steps, making them larger. As our axes
struck, the ridge vibrated for some considerable distance,
causing additional alarm and discomfort to Warwick as he
sat there in his icy saddle. Derek and I followed the other
pair, leading through. As I sat in the belay positions with
my crampons dug into both sides of the ridge, I felt the
clean, airy feeling of being high in space. Looking down over
the toes of my boot my eyes followed the glistening, plunging
lines of the ice down to the glacier below. The fall and sweep
of it drew the eye down, and for a moment I felt its dreadful hypnotic effect loosening the grip of balance and nerve,
impelling the fascinated mind and body downwards to follow those descending lines, to fall and fall, free in space. I
looked up quickly and the spell was broken.

We progressed more slowly than the others as we labored
over the step-cutting. By the time we had negotiated two
small gendarmes Warwick and Donald were out of sight in
the mist which had begun to shroud the mountain. Ahead
lay broad slopes up which we plodded slowly, sinking deeply
into the snow. Just below the summit the others had waited
for us, and together, side by side, we climbed the last slope
to the top.

We stood on the snow dome of the summit peering vainly
into the mist, which robbed us of a view which might reveal
the problems of the summit ridge of Carpe, or some of the
secrets of the ground over which we were to travel. We
stayed for about half an hour photographing each other
and eating slabs of cheese delicately split by Donald with
his ice axe. He was cook for the day. Warwick, from a secret
pocket, produced a small flask of whisky and we toasted our
success. After anointing the summit in the customary way
we started the descent.

On the ridge during the traverse, although moving safely,

I felt again, in my elephantine footwear, a loss of touch, a loss of that feeling of oneness with boots and crampons which is so essential on ice. My climbing was unsure and hesitant. I saw the impatient, superior looks of the others. The sickness of inadequacy and depression rose in my stomach.

When we were halfway across the broad plateau snow started falling fast, in big, whirling flakes, obliterating our old tracks and filling the steps of the pair in front. Just above the rock step the clouds cleared suddenly and we saw the curving rim of the col. I was struck by the precarious position of our tent, jutting on its small platform from the face which swept down to the wavering line of the bergschrund. Mist blotted out the scene as suddenly as it had appeared, and we blindly finished the descent in driving snow with the first signs of weariness damping our movements and slowing our steps.

It was midday when we took our crampons off and wormed into the tent. Inside was a confusion of sleeping bags, food, clothing, stove, and pots. In brewing tea we produced more disorder. The temperature rose and the snow continued to fall. Water seeped through the tent walls. We became very irritable and bawled each other out for touching the sides, but in the cramped space it was impossible to do otherwise. The floor became an oozing morass. We sat hugging the diminishing dry areas, occasionally catching glimpses of Carpé—when the mist cleared—through the open door. The warmth and the continually falling snow would make an attempt on the mountain impossible. We had to climb it that night, or go down. The crevasse incident had robbed us of a day on the col and we only had food for the next 24 hours, plus an emergency ration. The important question was, would it stop snowing in time and freeze up?

At three o'clock Donald began to cook supper, and just

as he was about to make the coffee I committed the ultimate of crimes by knocking over the billy of hot water. Unable to move, we watched the water invading our sleeping bags. No one said very much, but their looks drove me deeper into my corner and the meal was eaten in silence. Two hours later, having performed our contortionist's routine, we lay down, sardine-packed, to sleep. We were awakened by the alarm at midnight to find the snow still falling heavily. The temperature was above freezing point. We turned over in our pools of water and went back to sleep.

The bucking of the tent, in a gusty wind, made me open my eyes to be greeted by the sight of Derek snoring, openmouthed and unshaven. I lay watching the moisture streaming down the walls of the tent, each gust of wind sending a fine spray over us. Oh joyous morn! The others came to life with a repulsive chorus of grunts, groans, and breaking of wind. We withdrew to the back of the tent while Donald cooked breakfast in a minute clearing near the door.

We discussed at some length—somewhat heatedly, repeating all the old arguments—whether it was worth making an attempt on Carpe that night. Lack of food was the deciding factor. We could now only hope that descent would be possible. Some order was produced in the tent and we lay down to read, or sleep. No one could move unless the other three adjusted their positions, and in our discomfort and frustration we became even more bad-tempered.

Warwick was in a sarcastic mood and had referred to the crevasse incident several times as though it was my fault. To make it worse, when he moved—which he did often—he invariably kicked me in the face, or knocked the book from my hands. I began to attribute these accidents to a malevolent design of Warwick's to annoy me. *He may be big but he's got too much damned room.* How I hated him, sprawling his great form into my hard-gained pre-

serve of floor space and thrusting his vile-smelling feet into
my face. I gave up reading and lay there thinking murderous thoughts, not daring to voice my anger in an already
highly charged atmosphere. I fell into the miserable trap
of introspection.

*In the mountains over fourteen days . . . "fiddling about,"
Donald had called it. A third of the expedition gone and all
we'd done was travel a few miles of glacier and climb one
virgin peak. Why hadn't I brought up extra food? Here we
were, in a position to climb Carpé—probably a good day
tomorrow—and not enough food. I wasn't doing too well at
leading this show. What were the others thinking about the
crevasse business? I should have taken more care with that
blundering oaf Warwick . . . and my performance in those
bloody boots . . . Oh hell! Was it worth it?*

Warwick's feet came over again. The stench of sweat and
wet wool was suffocating. I pushed them off irritably. "Keep
your blasted feet out of my face, you're taking up half the
tent."

"Yes," said Derek. *Thank goodness for an ally. Pity you
didn't bend his car a little more,* I thought maliciously.
"You're a bloody nuisance. As long as Deacock's comfortable nothing else matters."

"Oh shut up," Warwick snarled back, "you don't realize
how difficult it is for me."

God! Difficult for him! How I hate his whining!

With disgusted groans we went back to our reading.

At lunch time we made as much room as possible in the
tent for Warwick, who was cook for the day. Derek lent a
hand to speed the cooking, so that we could all the sooner
spread ourselves once more. Unfortunately he burned his
hand on a hot billy and knocked the stove off balance. The
water slopped over and drenched Warwick's sleeping bag.

"Bloody hell, man!" roared Warwick. "What are you doing?"

Stung by the raised voice and ever sensitive to reproof from Warwick, Derek hurled back, "Every time I do anything wrong you always moan like hell. I'm damned if I'll help you again."

He still held the stove upright.

"I think it would be better if one of us cooked, not two," said Warwick coldly.

"Blast you then." Derek let go the stove, leaving it teetering dangerously. Warwick just managed to save the billy from falling. We ate another meal in silence.

Later in the afternoon the mood of pessimism, which had overtaken me in the morning, once more pressed upon me. Would we justify ourselves and the expedition? "You know," I said, voicing aloud the rationalization of my thoughts, "we'll have done well if we only climb one peak, do our scientific work and explore the glacier."

The others, especially Donald, looked surprised at my lack of normal optimism, but halfheartedly agreed. Donald nagged on, urging an attempt on Carpé and then a race down to the glacier with no food. In my frustrated and depressed state I longed to side with him, to say, "Yes, let's go tonight." Derek and Warwick, I knew, would then have swung over to the same opinion, but I argued against him. With no food, any holdup or mishap on the descent might develop quickly into a disaster.

Divided in our opinions, we grew apathetic, and one by one fell asleep in our sodden bags. We ate breakfast at eleven that night and emerged into a frozen, silent world. In such conditions an attempt on Carpé was just possible. Why not drop everything and try it? The thought was tantalizing but unrealistic. The world was hushed, frozen into utter stillness. We struck the tent, moving quietly, not speaking, as if hesitant to break this deep, complete peace. The soft light glowing down threw long black shadows contrasting sharply with the whiteness around us, and out over the tundra, beyond the Muldrow, the sky was a deep purple. Ribs of mountains, newly clothed with snow, probed out into the blue-green of the swamp and bog in which the lakes shone like small mirrors set in velvet. It was a scene that could hold one forever in a timeless silence, when even the mountains, gripped in the deep cold, had lost their awfulness, displaying only the beauty of their form.

We turned away reluctantly and cramponed down in long zigzags, crossed the bergschrund and descended into the upper bowl of the glacier. Here the snow lay like a feathery carpet. We ploughed cautiously on, past our old campside and the almost fatal gaping crevasse. The journey through the top tiers of the ice fall had lost some of its terrors. We found a corridor seamed with small crevasses which took us farther down, circumventing the traverse. Derek in the lead came onto a sloping shelf of hard, rough ice and ventured out, still in showshoes. With a wild, uncontrolled scuffling of feet he fell and shot down the slope. After twenty feet I held him and he dug his axe pick in. The sight of him dangling there, looking, in his woolen hat, like a furious gnome, struck me as so funny that I burst out laughing. The others joined in. When I could control myself I asked, "What happened Derek?" I was very polite.

"Can't you see I slipped?"

"Why didn't you put on crampons?" asked Donald.

Infuriated, and helpless, Derek roared, "Because I thought you might all moan at the delay."

"But you're the leader, Derek, you should decide, and we'll obey," said Warwick in a sickly, patronizing way.

"There are too many blasted leaders in this party. Pull me up, you grinning idiot Mills."

"Steady now, boy," we chorused from our superior position; then I hauled him up. Warwick took over the lead, for it was his turn, and we put on crampons.

"Too bloody late now," said Derek as we moved out onto the ledge. It soon petered out and merged with a vertical wall of ice which rose up on our left for about thirty feet. We cut ledges and secured ourselves while Warwick began the ice climb. Loaded as he was with his pack, holding with one hand on tiny incut holds, and cutting with the other, it was an example of balance climbing on ice of a very high standard. In spite of the fact that the ice was not solid and crumbled under pressure, he moved deftly and surely, his body well out from the ice, the rope falling perpendicularly. At two crucial points he hammered in pitons, the ring of metal on metal echoing among the *séracs* below us. The climb took him almost half an hour and not once did he stop for rest. It was as though he was proving finally to himself that he had recovered his nerve. He disappeared over the top and Derek followed, then Donald, each man finding the climb more difficult in the crumbling steps, with insufficient time to improve them. When my turn came I found the wall acutely difficult. I had to remove the pitons on the way up and was grateful for some robust assistance from the rope.

When I reached the top the other two, having gone off on a separate rope, were well down the avalanche debris. With Donald leading at a cracking pace we raced down in their tracks. On the snow slope, beyond the bergschrund, the four of us once more joined together on a single rope. Before beginning the crossing of the glacier we stripped down to shirtsleeves, for it was almost eight o'clock and the heat was already intense. When I started off in the lead I found that the glacier had undergone more changes and our early route could not be recognized. I tracked this way and that, seeking the safest path. My goggles misted up, so I took them off. In the blinding glare, with the sweat running into my eyes, I found it difficult to see the hidden crevasses. I probed every step.

"Keep a tight rope here, Warwick, it's a bloody great bridge and I'll have to move fast."

"O.K., got you."

"We'll have to jump this one, give me plenty of slack."

"Got a good belay? This one seems to twist all over the place."

Out there in front I was in a world apart from the others. All my nerves and senses concentrated on avoiding the hidden traps. My ears were alive to every noise. I could hear the rope running round Warwick's axe, as he belayed me, and its sibilant slithering across the snow. From all around me came the small protesting murmurs of the snow crystals as they surrendered to the sun.

Each faint shadow and change of texture in the snow, which might mark a crevasse, was patiently investigated. Having defined the limits of a crevasse I would pause and straighten up to bring some relief to my back, which ached abominably from the load and the constant bending and stretching. Then a step across, or a gently gliding tiptoe over the large bridges. Once safe, I would wipe the sweat away and turn to protect Warwick. So the intense routine went on.

"Right, come on, watch the edge, it slopes down."

Probe and move, probe and move. A few shuffling yards gained in as many minutes. It was a desperate journey—the worst glacier work yet.

The glacier creaked and groaned beneath our feet, like a dragon's wrinkled back writhing under the sword stroke of heat. Occasionally there would come from below an enormous, spreading, reverberating roar. It was as though we were walking across the ceiling of some great dome, from which one by one the chandeliers were crashing to the floor. At every booming explosion I felt certain that the particular part of the "ceiling" on which we stood must cave in and precipitate us into the vault below.

In mid-glacier we halted to change the lead and Warwick took over. As we clipped ourselves into new positions we heard the SA-16 overhead and soon it came into sight, flying up the glacier. Warwick spoke into the radio, but there was no reply.

"It's gone U/S," said Warwick, shaking it vigorously. We changed batteries with no result. The machine droned round, climbing from the glacier to search the col and ridge of Tatum and Carpe, patiently circling this way and that like a bird seeking its straying young. We watched helplessly as the amphibian turned away from us to the east and was lost behind the mountains.

"Now I suppose they'll get worried and send a rescue party. Blast the radio and the aircraft!" cursed Warwick, stuffing the set back into his kitbag.

The last lap across the glacier was just as difficult and nerve-straining as my stint. After nine hours without a rest we were tiring. I could see the stress of leading in Warwick's movements. Derek suddenly dropped into a totally unsuspected crevasse, his kitbag jamming when only his head was still above glacier level. Just afterwards I fell when jumping a small fissure, cracking my goggles and cutting my forehead, temporarily stunning myself. The accidents were the danger signs of fatigue, and our relief was considerable when we crossed the gaping chasm—now a little wider— and jerked off our packs by the two tents. It was like coming home.

10. Journey
to Raven's Camp

THE ENTHUSIASM of everyone for a rest day was eloquent evidence of our tiredness. Committed as we were to resting by day, in the heat of the sun we found sleeping difficult. For over a week our hours of good sleep had been, on the average, less than four a night. This and the load-carrying made inroads on our strength, and rest days were now essential to restore our reserves. It was a problem from which there was no escape at the low level of the glacier. No one could foresee just how much we were to suffer from lack of sleep in later days.

After breakfast we relaxed in the hot sun and slowly overhauled our kit. Derek fell asleep wearing only a pair of trousers and his string vest. In an hour the sun had produced the pattern of squares on his body. Donald sat with his binoculars focused on the ice fall, exclaiming each time an avalanche roared across our old track down into the bergschrund. We had beaten them by only two or three hours.

The day passed pleasantly, and in the evening Derek cooked a large pemmican curry which included dried bananas, raisins, butter, Marmite, dried onions, and dried potatoes. Even that mixture failed to kill the powerful taste of the pemmican. Tinned pears followed, then cake and coffee. We sat around in the Meade after supper, sipping our whisky lemon toddy, warm, relaxed, and pleasantly weary. Once more we enjoyed each other's company, talking and laughing over the incidents of the past few days.

"You know, down that crevasse it was like sitting in the bottom of a dark green bottle with the hole at the top like the opening of the neck."

"I thought you'd had it there, Warwick. I couldn't see a thing when I looked down."

"When I saw Jimmy's feet in those boots coming up the ridge I thought, so that's how an elephant climbs."

"Pity we didn't try Carpé. It would have gone on a good night like the one we came down."

"Yup, but it would have been tearing the arse out of it with only one Horlick's 24-hour bar each."

"Damn good scoff, Derek, but I didn't like those dried bananas, they remind me of monkey's fingers."

"They remind me of something else too—and less pleasant."

"Don't be such a dirty, old, Scottish doctor."

"Look, stop calling me doctor—my name's Donald. How would you like it if I called you captain all the time?"

"We'd love it, doctor; shows respect."

"Bloody English."

"Steady, you old Gaelic monster."

Then—wonderful, dreamless oblivion for twelve hours in the seductive folds of the sleeping bag. We awoke to find a fresh fall of snow and the mist low around us. The snow lay patchily on the rocks, contrasting with the drabness of moraine slag heaps, making our campsite look even more dreary and miserably untidy. The temperature was high—about 35°F—and through the mist from across the glacier came the crash of avalanches. Even Donald conceded that had we spent another day on the col to attempt Carpe, we would have been badly caught out on the return.

During the rest of the morning we packed the sledge and wrote up our diaries. After a fortnight in the mountains we had become an effective team and we now knew how best to operate under the prevailing conditions and circumstances. There were bound to be upsets between us, but I had expected them. They were only short-lived, and the potentially more serious antagonism between Derek and Warwick was fast fading. When there was work to be done, or a problem to be solved, all the diverse skills and intelligence of the party sprang immediately and single-mindedly together. There was no doubt about our ability to travel and climb where we wished, and the scientific work was proceeding well.

That afternoon, as on the previous rest day, we found time to catch up with the work. Donald worked away at his medical notes, occasionally asking questions about how we felt, and about our dreams. Under his direction we also filled in our questionnaires on food intake and activity for the past few days. He was tireless in keeping up with his medical work, forcing us to eat and drink when we were too tired to bother and taking temperatures and pulse rates whenever the opportunity arose.

No longer did we find it unusual, or annoying, to calculate in exact detail each ounce of our food eaten, or measure with Donald's graduated mug every drop of liquid swallowed. This was an essential part of our plan, to carry out the longest and most exact study yet undertaken of the calorific intake and provisioning of an expedition in the field. I was the only one not eating the full ration. It irked the others, who were always hungry, to see my leftovers being put back into the central pool, but they were not yet allowed to eat more than the ration.

Warwick sat outside the tent dressed in windproofs against the chill breeze, writing up the backlog of his "met" (meteorological) record from the notes in his diary. Wherever we went he carried a set of thermometers with which he took various readings at fixed times daily. He also noted wind speeds and directions, measured snow fall, and wrote long descriptions of cloud formations. Sometimes, when he thought he had established a pattern of conditions which produced a certain type of weather, he tried to forecast—not always successfully—what we could expect the next day.

Inside one of the tents I sorted, cleaned, and labeled rock-specimens collected on the col at Tatum. Derek was engaged in cataloguing exposed film and checking over his shooting list. The term "rest day" was, in fact, a misnomer.

In furtherance of the geographical objectives my plan was to push on to the head of the glacier, setting up two camps on the way. Having reached the head we would try to ascend the cirque of peaks which enclosed it; then, by way of a col, cross over to the other side with the intention of traveling a week or more in the unexplored country beyond. If this was not possible we hoped to climb the peaks on either side of the col and also gain a large plateau to the east. From there an exploratory journey might be undertaken.

Just after one o'clock in the morning, with half of the stores and equipment on the sledge and our backs, we buckled on the harnesses once more. Derek, the first man, cast around for a way out onto the glacier, but there was not one over which four laden men pulling a sledge could go. Sometimes the sledge was worth perhaps four porters, at others it was a hindrance. This was such a time. We could take it nowhere. In the heat of the two preceding days snow bridges had collapsed leaving gaping crevasses so wide as to be impossible. The glacier was changing fast, and even those bridges which remained were of soft, yielding snow.

We took off our harnesses and packs and, splitting into two parties, went off in opposite directions in an attempt to find a route out. Every way Derek and I turned we were brought up short by enormous offshoots of the great crevasse which almost encircled the camp. Time and again we would cross small crevasses only to be barred by this cavernous monster or unsafe snow bridges which we could not cross. Four hours later, at the remaining tent on the campsite, we all met together. The others had been no more successful.

"It looks as though Fred's crevasse has got us," said Warwick. We had coined this name when we had first found it. We were all depressed, feeling that the glacier, with stealthy malevolence, had trapped us while we rested. Derek reminded us of the glacier "road" we had seen out in the center, when crossing to the ice fall. Donald suggested that if we could find a route to it and then back-pack the stores out to a dump actually on the "road," we might cut our losses. If it froze up that night we could get away to a quick start, making full use of good conditions.

The reconnaissance proved successful, and while the others ferried out the kit I cooked a meal. Finally the empty sledge was towed out, packed, and left on some safe ice in the center of the glacier "road." Even this minor success did not alleviate our general gloom and irritability. We felt frustrated, eager to sledge away, impatient at the time slipping by.

It was now June 13 and we had spent nineteen days in the mountains. Nearly half our time gone and not a quarter of the work accomplished. *After all the effort of getting here, to Alaska, was it all to be for nothing? Was the expedition to fail in its aims?* The thoughts nagged at me; doubts dragged my morale down to bitter despondency. *There must be a freeze-up tonight! We must get on!*

Through the lowering clouds the unmistakable throb of the SA-16's engine broke in on my thoughts.

"Hello. British mountaineering party calling. British mountaineering party calling. Can you hear me, over."

There was no reply; the aircraft droned on.

"I cannot hear you. Radio is not working properly. We are still opposite ice fall, but proceeding up the glacier. In 72 hours' time we will be near the head. Over."

No reply again, but a moment after my transmission the plane flew off. Perhaps they could hear us; but if they couldn't and sent a rescue party that would be the complete end. It was too depressing to think about. The certain knowledge that time was flowing on, leaving us snared by the glacier, unable to take the opportunities it offered, rankled in my mind, making me resentful and withdrawn from the others. We went to bed early with the air balmy and warm and the clouds hanging low. In our sleeping bags we lay listening to the crash of avalanches and the groaning and roaring of the glacier as the heat encompassed its ruin.

During the evening the temperature had dropped and the next morning the snow was rock-hard. It was almost two o'clock when, with Donald leading, we threw our bodies forward into the harnesses and the sledge slid forward. With a perfect gliding surface, conditions were ideal for sledging. I felt superbly fit and for the first time, in the rear position, I reveled in the physical labor of sledge hauling. Donald, out in front, led skilfully, and with secure snow bridges there were few tedious halts. Everyone was in high spirits, and at occasional stops Derek wrote rude messages to me in the snow with his axe point.

It was a glorious morning. The sun, unseen by us behind the mountain wall, tinged with a delicate pink the tops of Carpé and Tatum and the ramparts of McKinley, endowing them with an ethereal grace that made their vastness less awesome. In contrast to the summits the lower snows glowed softly, like ivory. Before our steady progress the view of the wall-like cirque enclosing the upper Traleika unfolded slowly and majestically. Soft white clouds spilled gently over the icy battlements.

We had our lunch at four o'clock on the last patch of stones on the glacier, Warwick in his whimsical way erecting a sign consisting of a route-flag cane stuck through a ration-pack cover, which bore the words "Fred's Snack Bar." Beyond "Fred's" we twisted this way and that among small *séracs* and a tangle of crevasses. Over one stretch Derek lay on the sledge filming a "sledge-eye" view of our march. In the center of the *sérac* we convoyed him forward to a large ice block which provided a good viewpoint. We then retraced our steps to the sledge and started forward again while he filmed our progress towards the camera.

As we drew opposite him we were forced to cross a large and nasty snow bridge which sloped at a considerable angle. Here, while Donald and I were busy negotiating the crevasse, Warwick had, with considerable effort, pulled the sledge up the ramp towards him in anticipation of our next move. Unfortunately our move took him by surprise— so much so that he let go of the sledge, which slid majestically down again. Warwick, with his labor reduced to naught, turned ferociously to curse Donald and me, but as he did so the sledge arrived at the full extent of its rope and with a jerk spun him back again. With frightening violence he thundered on at us and at the sledge, with a commendable fluency of vile oaths, appealing to the mountains and some unseen being who floated just above his head. This altercation, and the uncontrolled laughter of Donald and myself, Derek recorded faithfully on celluloid. He continued filming us, against the magnificent backdrop of the mountain walls, until we were merely tiny dots on the enormous white expanse of the glacier. We then returned over a half mile or more to escort him back to the sledge. So we suffered in the name of art.

We toiled on up the long incline of the glacier where it swung right beneath the long flank of Pegasus Peak. The sun's brilliance, flung at us from each reflecting white wall, burned and blasted like a furnace. The sledge dragged; every step was hard-won in the softening snow. The mind sank back and the eyes merely contemplated the man in front and the snowshoe patterns underfoot. At last we reached the top of the slope, selected a campsite amid old avalanche debris, and put up the tents.

Warwick and I stamped out in the snow messages for the aircraft should it come over. The heat of the sun finally drove us to seek the shelter of a groundsheet which the practical Derek had rigged between the tents. Again sleep would not come, and even at six in the evening we were all still awake. Because of this I put our reveille back from nine until ten-thirty. This minor change of plan produced an argument over the starting time. Irritable by reason of un-satisfactory dozing, and overheated, we wrangled with each other. Undoubtedly the best working hours were between eleven at night and seven in the morning, but lately our starts had been delayed, forcing us to contend with bad conditions in the latter stages of the day's work. It was vital, however, to get sufficient sleep. Our waking hours numbered usually about eighteen, during most of which we were under-taking some sort of activity. Donald conjectured as to how long we could go on at this rate without proper sleep. He came to the conclusion that either 24 hours were not enough, or that we must have rest days more often.

The journey back to Crevasse Camp, for the second load, was slowed up by frequent halts to repair our snowshoes, which were all severely worn. Snow conditions were, however, very good and we arrived at three-thirty. After lunch we left the forlorn-looking campsite and jumped for the last time over Fred's crevasse.

The last two hours of the return were a killing, sweat-drenched drudgery despite the well-worn track. In the rough granulated snow the sledge wallowed like a top-heavy barque, building up a bow wave which we frequently had to stop and clear. The light plastic sledge was not built to take the heavy loads we hauled. It was designed to take a maximum of two hundred pounds and our usual load was at least three hundred. When overloaded it was difficult and exhausting to haul for its boat shape presented too much area to the snow. We had left in Aldershot a six-foot Nansen sledge which I now thought would be preferable to the one we were dragging. The Nansen was probably more delicate, but I was sure that we could have pulled bigger loads on it, and moved faster. We slogged on, tired and desperately hot, the sweat drying in salt rime on our faces. Derek, who had gone ahead, filmed our arrival.

Around the pile of food boxes there was an untidy mess of bits of food and tattered scraps of paper. A hole had been torn by some beast or bird in one of the outer covers, and two army snow rations were almost completely eaten. Whatever the creature was, it had ripped and torn up paper, strong cardboard, and plastic packaging with a furious strength. After a while we discovered the tracks of a large bird and Donald suggested that it might be an eagle. One thing was certain: with this unknown menace abroad we would in future have to keep food buried, or under cover. I wondered about our cache at Helicopter Camp. Washburn had warned me about bear and wolverine. It looked as though we might need our five days' spare rations dropped in. Standing next to our camp was a large ice block —probably a relic of a large avalanche—and with our axes

Derek and I hollowed it out to form a cache. It was hard work and took us over two hours, but in the end we had a safe larder for our food.

There remained several things to be done before we set out for the col. We were still too far away from it to make the journey in one day with heavy loads, yet the intermediate camp would not be a full day's journey away. Donald also wished to do some medical tests, and we all wanted to "have a look round all the corners" as Warwick put it.

There was one interesting corner which particularly intrigued us. Beyond Pegasus Peak and hidden by one of its spurs, the glacier appeared to begin rising steeply. We all cherished the faint hope that this would lead to a col between Pegasus Peak and McKinley. If this was so, it would give access to Pegasus and possibly to the great mountain itself, thus proving my contention that there must be a route up McKinley from the Traleika. It was an exciting thought.

To enable us to meet all these requirements we decided on a compromise. We would establish a dump at the foot of the col which would mark the site of the intermediate camp. At the same time we would be able to make a short reconnaissance of the supposed "McKinley col." Afterwards there would still be sufficient time for the medical work. Looking back at it now, I cannot understand why we decided against establishing a camp instead of just a dump; as things turned out it was as well that we did not.

We packed the sledge for the journey, and after making yet more repairs on our shattered snowshoes went to bed about six o'clock. After an hour of trying unsuccessfully to get to sleep I heard a fluttering of wings.

"It's that bloody bird," I whispered to Derek and quietly crawled out of the tent. A huge, black raven was slowly hopping away. Derek joined me and we threw some hard lumps of snow at it which all missed. The bird rose into the air and slowly flapped away across the glacier to disappear into a rock face on the far side. At least the mystery was explained, and we named the place Raven's Camp.

Derek went back into the tent, but I remained outside. It was the moment when the icy hand of cold begins to re-assert itself and halt the destruction of the usurping sun, freezing everything into immobility and imposing once again its will in a land where it is the supreme factor. With the onset of the cold came an enormous depth of silence broken only by the occasional whir of the anemometer spun by an errant zephyr. Around me, as I stood in the deep canyon of snow and ice, were the mountains, brilliantly white against the opalescent sky, the summits utterly re-mote. The upthrust of their might dwarfed me and filled me with humility. Could we ever attain them? Did we dare intrude upon this flawless communion of ridge and peak with space and sky? Even our small camp, with its warm aura of life, seemed to affront the cold, hostile world of the great glacier. The peace of the scene entered me and the uncanny silence was wrapped about me like a cloak. For a moment, all life was in perspective and my mind, divorced from the imprisonment of the body, moved timeless in the utter tranquility of space, in an ageless scene of absolute beauty. I felt uplifted, drained of all anxiety and fatigues, and I became aware of the deep happiness which filled my being. I do not know how long I stood there, but it was some time before the cold, creeping into my lightly clad body, brought me back to reality. Once in my sleeping bag I fell asleep almost immediately.

11. Journey
to the Glacier Head

FOR ONCE I rose quickly and was ready before the others. I strapped myself into the leading man's harness a quarter of an hour before they finally took up their positions in the traces. Quite irrationally I chafed at their slowness, and my fancied grievances against them came to the surface in the form of a sharp exchange with Warwick who, at the best of times, is not a man to be trifled with in the early hours of the day. Our tempers soon dissipated with the perfect going, and the light sledge came along easily. Ahead, the glacier rose steadily in a broad sweep. The crevasses were enormous. The depressions in the snow which marked their presence were sometimes over fifty feet wide, but the bridges were firm. We traveled, for once, almost lightheartedly with neither fear nor hindrance of movement.

Gradually we drew along the length of Pegasus to the point where we might see, on our right, the hoped-for col to McKinley. Each step opened up new vistas to us, revealing the hitherto unseen beauties of the glacier. At last we could see beyond the flank of Pegasus Peak, but there was no col. Instead, a thin serrated ridge—its fluted ice walls falling like a curtain to join the ramp of the glacier—met our eyes. It was a disappointment, especially to Donald, who dearly wanted to set foot on McKinley. The ridge did, however, join Pegasus Peak to the main massif of the great mountain and would be the key to any ascent from the Traleika. But a longer reconnaissance would be necessary to prove this and would have to wait.

By now the rays of the sun spread pink fingers across the glacier, staining the snow, and we gradually drew out of the shadows towards them. The gradient steepened and we zigzagged upwards until we reached a broad, level expanse near the foot of the col. Here we buried Quatermass —our large kitbag full of food and stores—marking its position with route flags. We sat on the sledge eating a snack and studied the route up the other col to the south, at the glacier head. It lay on the extreme left-hand side of the enclosing wall and seemed to be the only possible crossing place. The lower slopes, jutting out into the glacier, were shattered and riven by pressure into huge blocks of ice with towering, clifflike sides. Farther up there was a high step topped by a concave slope, its upper reaches rising very steeply to the jagged line of the col. It appeared possible to avoid the shattered area and the step, by moving up the glacier along the foot of the spur of the lower slopes. From this flank a steep traverse to the left would bring us out to the foot of the final section. This route had the added advantage of keeping well away from the enormous western face of a sharp-pointed peak rising from the left-hand side of the col. From the summit of this peak and its lower cliffs we could trace the black claws of avalanche trails, reaching across almost the entire slope below the col. In committee, by suggestion, countersuggestion, and close reasoning from all of us, the route was worked out and agreed upon. We estimated that from our present position it was a three-thousand-foot climb to the top and in good conditions we could make it in a day.

We returned quickly to Raven's Camp, Warwick using

the sledge as a toboggan down the long slopes. We were soon on the treadmill of the step test. It seemed much easier; probably our techniques were better. Relative fitness indices had improved in the case of Warwick, Donald, and myself, but Derek's remained quite steady, with scarcely any change since Aldershot. Our weights had hardly altered.

My appetite still continued to be "apathetic"—Donald's word—and I had yet to eat a full day's ration, while the others took in every scrap voraciously. In spite of our lack of sleep we were all very fit and only Derek gave Donald any cause for alarm. Every minor cut or scratch he sustained grew septic and his gums bled for a good deal of the time. Warwick also had trouble with his teeth. To counter this Donald had put them on a course of pills. This had been accomplished easily in the best sleeping-bag-side manner. "Do have these; they're lovely. I take them myself regularly."

Fortunately, Donald took every facet of his complicated task seriously. In camps he was forever melting snow in a black cape in order to provide a constant supply of water. He warned us, "You must keep up your fluid intake to at least six pints a day. Dehydration is fatal." From his small reservoirs he made copious quantities of orange and lemonade. He doggedly pursued experiments on his own person and I often saw him with a thermometer protruding from his mouth, apparently oblivious of its presence.

We went to bed hoping for a continuance of the good weather, but though the sky above the col was a clear, deep blue, far away to the north—perhaps over the McGonagall Pass—great purple banks of cloud were building up. It was a little cooler than in recent days, but I could not sleep; my mind was alive with the excitement of the exploration ahead. I found the greatest joy in mountains when traveling through them, rather than in struggling against one particular peak. All the skill and craft of mountaineering are needed and must be deployed to the full to meet the new problems and factors encountered every day, with every step. There is, too, the gradual unfolding of the country before one's eyes and the eager anticipation and never ending conjecture on what lies around the corner, or over the other side. The ascent or crossing of a pass, or col, is in every way as satisfying as a peak climbed. Perhaps even more so, for whereas on the summit the main task is over, on a pass there is the intriguing problem of crossing to the new country beyond. A way has been found: the freedom of the mountains is in one's possession. Even the view is as rewarding as one from a summit, and nearly always more satisfying, in its truer perspective, than looking down from a superior height on a tangle of peaks. All this, allied with some worthwhile scientific work, which will widen man's knowledge of himself and his environment, is a form of self-expression and a pursuit in life which can be wholly satisfying and creative.

I must have fallen asleep quite suddenly, for the next thing I knew the needle-sharp note of the alarm bell drilled through to my consciousness and I awoke to find the sides of the tent bellied in by snow, the cold cloth resting on my face. I looked out; visibility was nil and it was snowing heavily. I called to Warwick that there would be no move. Just before two o'clock I was roused by Donald's voice as he cursed softly outside. He had awakened to find the tent pressing heavily on his face, the weight of snow having snapped the guys. Barefooted and dressed in only pajamas and a vest he worked for nearly half an hour groveling in the snow to prevent the total collapse of the tent. Later, with Gaelic dourness, he said he had felt a little chilly.

At six-thirty I went into the third tent, which we used as

a store and kitchen, to relieve Warwick, who was already up melting snow. We were still cooking on the same system of one man each day and I crouched in the tent—the floor a soggy mess of melting snow and broken biscuits—cooking the porridge and weeping steadily because of the Primus fumes.

We spent the rest of the day leisurely, eating a ration bolstered up with food from our luxury box, and drinking everything from orangeade to Horlick's. Mostly we wrote up diaries and read our books. Derek had a collection of Somerset Maugham stories reverently compiled by an American admirer of the "Master" and a similar compendium of Noel Coward's works. Both these books were in constant demand as light relief from the heavier works. *War and Peace*—which seems to be the book taken on most expeditions—had been brought by Donald. He delighted mostly in its stories of the graft, intrigue, and internal politics of the Tsarist armies. These scenes of Russian military life he gleefully compared with similar examples in the present-day British army, reading out large selections to prove his point, mainly for the benefit—and, he hoped, to the annoyance—of Warwick and myself. Warwick was reading Herodotus; ever keen to reduce the weight he carried, he tore out and threw away each page as he read it. Some future traveler on the Traleika may reap the benefit of this serialization. My main reading was the *Legacy of the Ancient World,* an evaluation of the culture left to Western civilization by the Greeks, Romans, and Hebrews. I also carried a number of pamphlets which I studied in a desultory fashion in preparation for the Staff College entrance examination in the coming February. I often commended myself for my professional zeal. Remarkably enough, I passed the examination. This reading formed our main intellectual exercise and an escape from each other.

When they were tired of reading, Derek and Donald played chess. Then Warwick contested Derek in a game of "Battleships." This ended in an argument when Warwick won and Derek found that he had been playing on a much larger expanse of paper with an enormous numerical superiority in ships!

I felt again the loss of time weighing heavily upon me, but Donald was delighted with this unexpected rest. The snow stopped for a moment and then started again.

Derek in my tent roared out, "It's snowing again." There was a resounding cheer from the other two.

"You keen boys," I jeered back.

"If I can get four more hours' rest, I'll do anything for you, Jimmy," cooed Donald.

From Warwick came snatches of zany song, each verse of which ended with the words, "Put your feet on the table and have a little nig nog with me." After several stanzas he was told to put his feet elsewhere.

There were bursts of conversation between the tents interspersed with long silences. Occasionally, like an eavesdropper, I would hear talk in the other Meade.

"Doctor, you're scrunching. Stop scrunching Spangles in my ear," whined a peevish Warwick.

There was no reply. Suddenly I heard a rending belch.

"These vile pills of yours, doctor, they're crippling me."

This was too much for Donald.

"Be thankful they're not Army ones. They'd fix you properly," he cracked back.

Derek and I worked out some future film sequences and then asked for suggestions from the others. This gave Warwick his chance.

"What about that bit when you fell down the ice slope wearing snowshoes, Derek?"

Derek, smarting under this, said, "We could do Deacock in the crevasse."

"Balls," replied the ever polite Deacock briefly. The conversation lapsed again.

The crash of avalanches went on all the morning and into the afternoon. We were very mindful of the fact that we camped among old debris. Some of the enormous rushing crashes seemed so close that I could imagine the white wall of dust and ice rolling towards us. But none reached the camp.

In the late afternoon the mist cleared slightly, revealing the peaks floating above it, their height accentuated by this apparent disembodiment. Clouds never fail to enhance the mystery and appeal of the mountains, and with a furious clicking of camera shutters and whirring of the Bolex the scene was recorded. Almost two feet of snow had fallen and we dug the tents out. The walling up of the ice cave was then completed and the sledge packed, for we intended to try and move the next day, whatever the weather.

In deep snow and through thickening mist, in which it was impossible to distinguish gradients, we made the frightful haul up to the dump on the following day. Despite snowshoes we often sank up to our knees, the sledge running forward only a few feet at a time. After each pause it was necessary to fling ourselves forward in the harness time and time again to free the sledge from the entrapping snow.

At Terminus Camp, as we called it, we pitched two tents, and unearthed Quatermass. We had decided to take enough food to allow us to stay out for ten or eleven days if necessary. In addition to five days of the Army snow ration and two days of normal expedition rations, Donald and I made up four days' special light ration, weighing just over a pound, which we called the KINMIL pack. It consisted of the following:

	Ounces
Porridge	$1\frac{1}{2}$
Kendal Mint Cake	2
Horlick's Fudge (concentrated emergency food)	2
Energade (glucose drink)	$\frac{3}{4}$
Nut pemmican	2
Soup powder	$\frac{1}{2}$
Chocolate	2
Orangeade	2
Sugar	4

It was customary to issue rations to the cook in two-day lots, as they were packed that way, and this control of rationing was Donald's job. The cook retained only the main items for cooking, issuing out to each man his personal ration of chocolate, hard biscuits, sugar, and sweets. These were kept in a personal "goodies" bag and could be eaten at will. With these tasty items self-control was essential, for by now the other three felt hungry most of the time. The stage had been reached when Derek, for one, sulked all day because he had lost the toss over chocolate and received a plain bar instead of the hoped-for milk block. Envy flickered up when someone else received acid drops, or mints, which were rated much higher than fruit sweets. We all looked with sharp attention when the sugar ration was counted out; an extra lump made a good deal of difference.

The loads were finally weighed out at roughly 70 pounds each. Derek confided in me that by carrying the same load he felt at a disadvantage in comparison with Warwick, who was at least thirty-five pounds heavier and who, in theory, could carry more weight. He was in fact voicing a secret fear that I am sure must trouble most mountaineers or travelers before setting out on a severe journey. It is the doubting of one's own ability to stand the pace—to keep up with

the others. One fears the stark comparison of his performance with that of others, fears that his best will not be good
enough, and fears, also, a breakdown which might throw a
dangerous strain on the party. This fear is often rational-
ized, and a man carrying a heavier load—even a few pounds
heavier—is likely to attribute his breakdown or his poorer
performance to this handicap. It is a grudging thought that
can nag away unbearably on a hard, exacting journey.

When we went to bed the mist was still down and it was
freezing. In any case, whatever the weather, we were determined to attempt the ascent to the col that night.

12. Ascent
to Charybdis Col

THE THICK MIST closed clammily around us as we left Terminus Camp. It was somewhat before midnight, and the phenomenon known as white-out—when the mist meets the snow, forming an impenetrable white wall—was at its worst. We could distinguish nothing ahead, and not even the snow beneath our feet was clearly visible. There was nothing on which to focus one's eyes. Gradients were distinguishable only because they were harder going. Route-finding was impossible. Searching for crevasses in the dim light and deep snow was sheer nerve-racking guesswork. The crust on the snow gave way with every step, and on slopes we slipped back half the distance of every pace forward. It was exhausting, slow work, and because no landmarks were visible we could not gauge our progress. All our faith was in the two compasses by which we navigated. Every so often, when beset and bewildered by a mesh of crevasses, we sat down in the snow straining our eyes, seeking some sign that would assist our route-finding, but we found none.

Just before four o'clock we crossed a huge crevasse by a spectacular snow bridge and then found, after some distance, that whichever way we turned further progress was barred by enormous chasms. Our defeat seemed imminent when suddenly the murk began to clear and soon the sun

broke through with the rosy light of early morning. We
stood on the top of a large *sérac* about the size of a football
field with precipitous cliffs on three sides. Fortunately our
navigation had been good and we were only a little distance
off our route, which we regained by retracing our steps.

I was, by now, in the lead and began the weary plod across
steadily rising snow to a steep slope below the traverse. The
snow beneath the crust was soft and powdery, accepting the
snowshoes and legs almost to knee depth. Each time, in
order to make a pace forward, the foot had to be raised
clear of the crust until the thigh was parallel with the surface. Down would go the foot to sink in again. In such going
I was capable of moving only in twenty-pace bounds. I
counted the steps, *one, two, three, four, . . . eighteen, nineteen, twenty,* then stopped to lean forward on the axe, gasping. Then on again, *one, two, three, four,. . . .*

At the foot of the slope I handed over to Donald, and as
the steep face was hard and firm we changed into crampons.
In long zigzags we climbed steadily. At the top we moved
left to come out on the slope looking down the Traleika.
Here we ran into fields of deep powder snow through which
we laboriously ploughed a deep furrow. Farther up the
ascent steepened, and it was necessary to change the lead
frequently as we floundered along waist-deep in lumpy
avalanche debris.

It was now almost eight o'clock and already it was hot
and airless in the brilliant sun. We had to stop soon—and
in a place protected from avalanches. After another half an
hour's slog we came upon a *sérac* which rose in the shape of
a banana with a flat top large enough for a campsite. It was
moated against avalanches by crevasses on three sides. On
this spectacular site we pitched our tent, the entrance facing
straight down the glacier. We were still only halfway up

to the col. The mist and adverse snow conditions had combined to kill our hopes of reaching it in one day.

We ate our lunch and, three hours later, our supper, sitting in the sun looking over the glacier. Our track stood out plainly, and with the glasses we could just see the single tents left at Terminus and Raven's Camp. Over the McGonagall Pass area the clouds were building up, just as they had done before the last snowfall. Warwick, with that dauntless confidence possessed only by meteorologists, predicted more snow.

Donald handed out sleeping pills, but before they took effect we discussed what we would do after completing our present journey. There would not be a great deal of time left, and we needed good weather if we were to attain all our objects. The first phase would be a speedy foray to explore the right-hand fork of the glacier. This might confirm the new route up McKinley and also offer a way up Pegasus Peak from a different flank. There was also the possibility of a col which might give access to Carpe and perhaps Mount Kaven. The second phase would be an attempt on Pegasus Peak from the Raven's Camp side—if no route was possible from the right-hand fork. An attempt on Carpe would be the third phase, and we intended to delay our withdrawal from the mountains as long as possible in the hope of fulfilling these plans.

I fell into a shallow sleep to be awakened by a jet throbbing overhead, quite low. The radio once again brought no answer. It was possible that they were looking for us, but we were too tired to care.

Donald awoke me about midnight—shattering a dream in which Jeanne and I were entertaining Colonel Reichert to tea. The alarm had failed to go off. We looked outside. A mist blanketed everything and snow was falling thickly.

The crash of frequent avalanches could be heard and we thought it prudent to stay put.

We lounged in our sleeping bags until noon, and for the first time on the expedition managed to hold a fairly serious conversation. We found it was a fascinating exercise to think of names for the two cols and the ice fall. On the col between Tatum and Carpe we bestowed the name of Waggoner's Col, in honor of my Corps, and for the ice fall, Albuhera Glacier for Warwick's regiment. The col above, because of the clouds which often seemed to whirl and swirl around it, we named Charybdis.

The talk ranged on from Communism to Catholicism to arguments about Parachute Brigade exercises—in which we had all taken part—and encompassed such other diverse subjects as the will to survive and Aleister Crowley, the "Great Beast" of modern black magic who had also been a mountaineer.

In the afternoon, when the mist had dissipated, we made a reconnaissance to a point from which we could see up to the col. The way was steep but fairly straightforward, and we could discover no difficult passages. By midnight we had trudged along our track to the limit of the reconnaissance. The mist slowly closed in upon us until, when we turned upwards, everything was again blotted out. From out of the north there came, completely unheralded, a rushing, shrieking, surging gale and with it a blizzard. Fortunately our backs were towards it. We moved doggedly on, in the midst of the turmoil of wind and snow, deafened by the gale's roar as it besieged the battlemented *séracs* defending the col above. The air was filled with flying pelletlike snow and we pulled our long hoods close around our faces to protect them from its rasping sting.

The ascent grew steeper, and as we climbed I could see

the boot soles of the man above me projecting from the
pigeonhole steps as though from a ladder. We groped our
way upwards, belaying each other carefully over crevasses which lurked like soft-mawed monsters in the deep
snow. The face seemed to go on forever, and at every step
we sank in up to our thighs. In the mist and the roaring
battle of the wind, we knew that beneath our feet was the
silent threat of avalanche. We were in a desperate position,
moving blindly, but retreat was equally dangerous; we had
to go on.

The gradient eased slightly, but the snow grew even
deeper. Derek, in the lead, was sinking in so much that he
could make no headway, so the taller Warwick took over
and struggled on. Out of the mist a white wall reared up in
Warwick's face, and we stood in the icy, swirling wind
watching him kick steps upwards to the right, the spume
flying with every lunge of his feet. The snow tore into us in
solid sheets, and by now our windproofs were ice-sheathed.
As we stood there, the wind snatching the breath from our
mouths, my mitts froze into the shape of my hands which
clutched the head of the ice axe. My beard was frozen solid
to the wool of my balaclava helmet, and an icicle hung from
one of my nostrils.

Suddenly, Warwick recoiled in horror from a void which
opened up at his feet. He could not move directly down,
for twenty feet below a crevasse yawned. Derek, who by
now was also on the face, belayed him carefully as he tried
to traverse right still further. When this proved impossible
Warwick decided to retreat, telling Derek to go down first.
Derek took two or three steps, then slipped, but Warwick
held him after he had fallen some ten feet. We watched
Derek as he hung for a few moments helpless against the
face, his feet kicking for a hold only a yard or so above the

open crevasse. Slowly he half climbed and was half pulled up to Warwick. They then climbed down safely and joined us.

I took the lead and moved left across more crevasses, wading waist-deep in the fine powdery snow, until I was brought up short by a bewildering maze of *séracs*. Donald cast around hopefully in another direction, but still upwards. In a few yards he was stopped by an abyss, on the other side of which he glimpsed briefly another, even higher, cliff.

The wind had risen in force, rushing through the channels between the ice cliffs like a demented banshee, tearing at them in its fury. We stood there bracing ourselves against it, debating in shouts, which could just be heard above the awful drumming roar, as to what we should do. The only wise thing to do was to camp until the storm ceased. Derek remembered a flat spot a few yards back, under a cliff, where we might pitch a tent. We retraced our steps and in the flying scud, with the tent flailing like a trapped animal, we made camp.

As soon as the tent was secured we piled inside. The others sat on their kitbags around the sides, watching with hungry eyes while I crouched in the center, heating up a thick hoosh of meat bar, Oxo, and tomato soup. We ate ravenously, our thawed clothes now clinging soggily to our bodies. The meal over, we cleared as much snow as possible from inside the tent; then, two at a time—for it was not possible for all to move at once—changed into dry clothes and got into our sleeping bags. Donald was last, struggling into his "John L. Sullivan" long white pants while sitting on Warwick and Derek. This was done rather overenergetically I thought as he bounced his long, angular body up and down on his two prostrate victims, whose appeals for mercy he answered with gleeful Scottish oaths. When he was finally in his bag he wriggled down to join us lying head to toe, more or less flat.

The tent bucked alarmingly like a live thing under the onslaught of wind and snow, the fabric rattling and crackling until we thought it must tear. Sheets of snow seemed to be hurled bodily at us, and gradually the tent grew darker as the drifts piled up around it. Despite our breathing and the heat of our bodies, ice began to form along the upper walls and the ridge of the tent. Donald, with his macabre sense of humor, told of a time when he had camped below the summit of Nevis in a storm, and the wind, in one huge swiping gust, had carried their tent away, leaving them staring up into the wild blackness of the night. We commented sarcastically on this cheerful Scottish anecdote and comforted ourselves with the thought that a tent made for Everest, and ballasted with over a quarter of a ton of inert humanity and kit, was not likely to sail away too easily. It was impossible to sleep through the deafening uproar of the wind and the occasional heart-stopping moments when the tent floor lifted and we felt powerless against the great force bearing in on us. So by common consent we brewed up again, and then with the aid of sleeping pills at last fell asleep.

13. *Charybdis Col*

THERE WAS no clearing of the mist the next day, and although the storm had abated, snow continued to fall. Climbing was out of the question. Indeed, after the storm and the snowfalls of the past six days, it seemed unlikely that we would get suitable conditions for some time.

In the early morning we dug the tent out, for it was almost buried, and retightened the guy ropes. To our horror we found that we were camped under a gigantic overhanging cornice, which rose above us like the prow of a ship. We realized that the maze of obstacles we had encountered the day before were a combination of crevasses, clifflike *séracs,* and cornices, which rose steeply from the col spreading in both directions, facing north and south. The one in our own back yard looked quite stable, and by driving pitons into it we were able to hang up our ropes and packframes.

Warwick and Donald set off on a reconnaissance to find the true col, while Derek and I continued with the domestic work. Because of our punctured air mattresses we had been for some time using flattened Royal Army Service Corps "compo" boxes laid between the snow and the tent floor cloth. The light fiberboard proved to be an excellent insulation, and we had carried some up to the col. Inside the tent Derek and I laid a mosaic of clothes-filled polythene bags, kitbags, and snow-ration covers. A bright pink, foam rubber bath mat, which Warwick used, completed the picture of gracious living.

The other two returned with the report that there was no proper col as such, only a small level gap between the cornices, which lay just over two hundred yards away to the west. Breaks in the mist had given them momentary views of precipitous ice and rock falling away on the other side. They were convinced that a descent to the far side was impossible; therefore, when the weather cleared our immediate objective would be the peaks on either side of the col. They did not return empty-handed, however, for scientific fervor had prompted them to collect some rock samples for me. It was a noble thought, but while it improved my collection it also increased the weight of my pack.

For the rest of the day we lay cramped in the tent reading, sleeping, and brewing up tea and lemonade by turns. Considering the fact that at most times if one man wished to move he required the consent of at least two others, we all remained remarkably polite. We debated whether or not it would have been a better idea to have brought two tents for this more protracted stay. The extra weight on the individual's back would have been about four pounds, but so sensitive were we to even one extra pound added to our packs, that we decided the discomfort of living in one tent was well worth it. Outside, the snow continued to fall.

From midnight onwards, at hourly intervals, Donald and I looked out at the weather. We could see nothing. Through the mist the great flakes of snow slanted down driven by a brisk wind. We could not face another day's idleness and so we made ready for an attempt of the adjacent peaks. Derek and Donald were to go to the west and Warwick and myself to the east. We roped up and started just after eight o'clock.

Warwick and I traversed the slope below the col, making

a slow course, knee-deep in snow. It was bitterly cold and the wind cut into our faces. The mist and snow hampered our route-finding, and for the journey back we left a trail of route flags in our wake. Turning upwards, we climbed steeply, crossed a large snow bridge, and began to ascend the slope beyond which led up to the ridge. From our view of the peak some days earlier, we vaguely recalled that this ridge might be followed to the summit.

As we gained the ridge—a narrow curving line in the mist —the wind struck us, sweeping up from the abysmal depths to our right, tearing at us in vicious gusts. We inched along from belay to belay, our windproofs plastered in an icy armor. At times I could scarcely see Warwick through the flying snow. The cornices flowed on like waves, bearded with icicles and jutting on both sides of the ridge. We trod a delicate path between them, the ridge rising in a series of sloping steps. Each time we topped one, another came into view. The ridge grew narrower until it was a delicate sawedge of snow and we squirmed along it with a leg on either side. To our right the mist swirled and hinted at the awful drop. We could almost physically feel the frightening gulf of space below.

The lead changed more frequently as we tired of the struggle against wind and deep snow. At one pause I looked back at Warwick. He stood hunched up and braced against the wind, his red windproofs ice-sheeted, and I could just make out his face peering from under the funnel of his anorak hood, icicles hanging from his beard. He bore himself, amid the wrath of the elements, with a patient, enduring acceptance.

A few yards on, the ridge flung itself upwards in a steep ice pitch. This took some time to overcome, and at one point there was an awkward, exposed step across, which could only be made when there was a lull in the wind. After twenty

Donald Kinloch and Derek Pritchard unload the helicopter after its second lift to Helicopter Camp.

The ridge of Tatum from Waggoners Col. Donald Kinloch and Warwick Deacock are seen on their way to the foot of the rock step.

Derek Pritchard and Donald Kinloch in the seracs of the Traleika and
Muldrow glaciers. In the middle distance, like a wedge driven into
the glaciers, is the long ridge of Mount Tatum. Farther up the
Traleika Glacier the sun lights the summit of Pegasus Peak.

Pegasus over the Traleika Glacier. A photograph of the expedition
flag taken at midnight.

The party on the West Face of Anniversary Peak. Above them the great summit cornices spread their long shadows down the face. The highest finger of the shadow is thrown by the summit itself. Beyond, and far below, although the camera makes it appear to be a continuation of the peak, is the large snow plateau. Thrusting up to the cornices of Anniversary Peak and the plateau is the precipice of the South Wall across which the traverse was made to gain the West Face.

Banana Serac Camp. Jimmy Mills and Warwick Deacock look on while Derek Pritchard enlarges the tent platform. Below, the Traleika Glacier sweeps away out of sight.

Warwick Deacock and Jimmy Mills on the slopes leading to the ridge of Anniversary Peak.

Derek Pritchard on the ice wall below the Notch. Above him, Warwick Deacock moves along the ridge towards the same point.

Ice. Derek Pritchard on the West Face of Anniversary Peak.

With Donald Kinloch in the lead, Jimmy Mills and Derek Pritchard return to Raven's Camp after the reconnaisance of the lower defenses of Pegasus Peak.

Donald Kinloch on the Notch of Anniversary Peak. Directly above his head, and beyond the jutting cornice, can be seen the "fishtail" on the ridge with the tracks leading over it. In the top left of the photograph is Mount Foraker.

Jimmy Mills climbing away from the Notch on the first part of the traverse under the cornices. The camera belies the steepness of the angle.

Derek Pritchard roping down the ice wall from the Notch. Below, beyond the bergschrund, Donald Kinloch operates the movie camera.

Warwick Deacock (seated), Derek Pritchard, and Jimmy Mills gaze down on the Traleika Glacier from the summit of Pegasus Peak.

Warwick Deacock looks at the route back along the Traleika Glacier. To the left is Mount Tatum.

The effect of the relentless freezing wind can be seen on Derek Pritchard (with camera), Warwick Deacock, and Jimmy Mills as they pose for Donald Kinloch on the summit of Pegasus Peak.

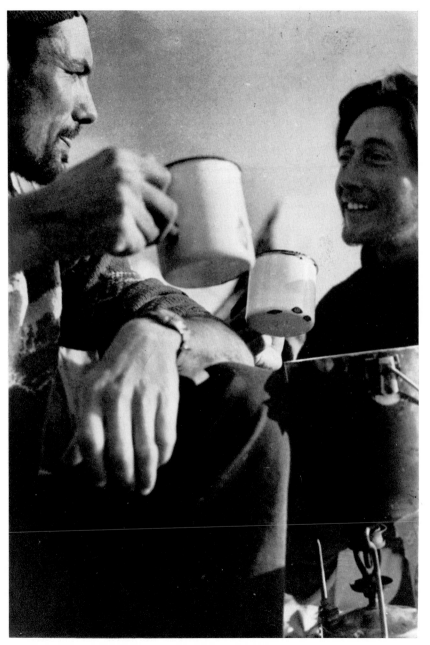

Warwick Deacock (left) and Jimmy Mills comparing the flavor of two of those well-known nighttime beverages.

Pegasus Peak—the return to the glacier. In the seracs and about to cross the ice bridge over the bergschrund. Behind is the rock wall which forms the base of the rock face.

A look back at Pegasus Peak during the march out. At the head of the glacier the lower slopes leading to Charybdis Col can be seen, but clouds blanket Anniversary Peak and Mount Staghorn.

In the somber setting of the old site of Creaking Camp, Jimmy Mills, Warwick Deacock, and Derek Pritchard finish off the last of the rations after failing to locate the food dump.

Escape from the Traleika Glacier.
One of the party roping down the
ice cliff.

In mid-Atlantic on the way home.
Left to right: Warwick Deacock,
Derek Pritchard, Jimmy Mills, and
Donald Kinloch.

feet the angle grew less. We clawed our way to the top, driving the picks of our ice axes in and hauling on them to pull ourselves upwards, while the wind battered at us, flinging sharp, needlelike ice particles into our faces and rattling them against our boardlike clothes. Beyond, the ridge continued in a single thin tracery of ice.

In these conditions it would be difficult enough to get back over our route, but this last obstacle imposed the limit. We had already passed beyond the normal margin of safety and to have gone on would have defied all the tenets of good mountaineering sense.

We turned back to fight our way down the ridge, in the unrelenting wind and entrapping snow, to find our tracks already filled and the flags almost buried. The campsite looked even more bleak and desolate when we trudged in; the tent was almost buried in the snow. Cries from the others of "Did you get up?" greeted us, together with the news that they had climbed their peak. Their climb had been up an exposed snow ridge which ended, near the top, in a maze of *séracs* and cornices. Finally they had struggled through these to find the summit was a wind-flung cornice up which they had to kick steps. They were delighted with this, the expedition's second virgin ascent—not including the two cols—and we toasted their success in steaming cups of tea.

Donald decided to name the peak Mount Staghorn. The name was suggested by the fact that when they had last climbed alone together, they had discovered on Ben Nevis a stag's body and had removed the horns. The name, which conjured up nostalgic memories of Scotland, delighted Donald immensely. It was one of his happier failings as a staunch Scot (and a source of amusement for Warwick and myself) that he would compare any scenery, or place, to some part of his native land. His observations on these like-

nesses were often couched in folksy Scots. Thus the vast
arena of the Traleika had become "the wee corrie" and the
enormous ramparts of McKinley were to his eyes "just like
the Ben." Warwick and I made the mistake of assuming that
this was lighthearted Scottish whimsy. But our leg-pulling
and facetious mangling of the Scottish tongue met only with
hard looks. The feelings of a Scot for his native land are obviously not to be trifled with. In sharp contrast to his normal dourness he could be quite volatile, and we often accused him of being rather more Gallic than Gaelic in temperament. He, on the other hand, condemned us as being
inhibited English.

By the evening the tent seemed almost completely
snowed under. Certainly the entrance was drifted right over
and it was too cold and too difficult to get out to relieve ourselves. Luckily, empty polythene fuel bottles proved useful receptacles although their narrow necks were potentially
dangerous.

We awoke at intervals during the night only to hear the
snow pattering against the few inches of roof still unburied.
The temperature rose, melting the icicles hanging from the
roof and the water dripped onto our faces and sleeping
bags. We all spent a thoroughly uncomfortable night full of
moans, groans, and irritable movement. Derek was the main
cause of the trouble; curled up in a ball like the dormouse in
Alice in Wonderland, he took up more than his allotted share
of space and pushed his hard bristly head into Warwick's
face. It was an extremely touchy Warwick who got up to
cook breakfast. The labor of digging his way out of the door
and finding the billies, which he had filled with ice the previous day, did nothing to sweeten his mood.

Donald continued to lie full length, pressed into the side
of the tent, with Derek and me sitting at the other end, still
in our sleeping bags, our knees pulled up under our chins.

For a moment the Primus stove burned low and weak— after many attempts by Warwick to light it—then began to flare violently, flames spurting up to the roof. Paraffin from a leaky valve also caught fire on the floor and the pool of burning liquid spread towards Donald. With remarkable agility and without bringing his hands out of the bag, he twisted sideways away from the flames, rearing up like a large green caterpillar. These antics, and Warwick's frenzied efforts to extinguish the stove, brought derisive roars of laughter from Derek and myself. These were not appreciated by the cook, nor by the Scots contortionist still thrashing about in his bag. Warwick's rate of swearing went up alarmingly, and our laughter died away abruptly as we too realized there was now a real danger of the tent's catching fire. Unaided, he at last managed to put out the flames. Paraffin fumes filled the air, making our eyes water and smart.

The lower half of the tent was almost clear, except for a bundle of Warwick's wet clothing in a corner, and in a space about two feet square he cooked breakfast. The visible part of the floor was crowded with mugs, mess tins, plates, and food. On the sides of the tent the wall bags were filled to overflowing with "goodies," binoculars, film, books, and medical kit; from one a stethoscope draped. Overhead, Donald's water bottle and mitts hung from the roof, together with a thermometer registering 56°F, while under some of the debris on the floor an alarm clock ticked away.

The Primus flared again and went out, hissing violently, adding more fumes to the foul atmosphere in the tent. Warwick shook the stove and found it empty, and so our tea and brose were made without the advantage of boiling water. When the breakfast had been dished out, Warwick crammed his great bulk onto us and we settled down to eat. By now we had lost all the finer eating utensils and simplicity was all. Donald, being more skilled than the rest of us in coping with this native dish, managed with a three-pronged fork. Warwick's dainty red plastic teaspoon looked almost effete compared with Derek's flattened tent peg. I had the only proper spoon. The others found my eating habits annoying. Not only did they watch hungrily while my store of un-eaten rations slowly grew, but I actually washed my mess tins and eating irons after each meal, sometimes between courses. Cissy! Later, unfortunately, I lost my reputation as a rather finicky paragon of cleanliness, when Derek discovered me washing my feet in my mess tins.

The meal over, aching behinds and cramped limbs made themselves felt.

"Could you move your shoulder a couple of inches, Derek, it's in my chest," pleaded Donald.

"I'm pinned by Warwick. What do you want me to do?" asked Derek.

"I just want you to sit up, that's all," and without further ado Donald raised himself with a monumental heave, thus settling the matter to his satisfaction and our added discomfort.

After another hour of this cramped agony in the vile atmosphere of the tent, we elected unanimously to emerge, if only for a reconnaissance. We dressed two at a time and slowly crawled out of the tent. It was not snowing, but the mist was dense and the white-out was absolute. There was the faint hope that we could get above it and at least see something of the country that lay around us. Any serious climbing was out of the question because of the dangerous snow conditions, so our efforts were to be limited. But anything was better than just sitting in the damp cavern in the snow that we called a tent, with time slipping away.

Our attempt was even more limited than we had expected. In twenty minutes we covered fifty yards and then came to a dead stop. Not even Warwick was able to force his way through the snow, which reduced the most vigorous efforts to ineffectual floundering. We returned once more, miserable and frustrated, to the wretched tent.

By digging away the snow which was pressing on the walls we made more room inside. Derek relaid the sopping floor, and in his usual enthusiasm for tidiness produced order in the tent. We carefully removed as much snow as possible from our clothes and boots before entering, and once inside we were able to sit or lie in some sort of comfort.

Periods of enforced idleness in mountains are often fruitful occasions to examine motives for climbing—especially at times like this, when one finds little joy in one's companions or in the mountains. The classic and oft-quoted answer given by Mallory to a question on why he wanted to climb Everest—"Because it is there"—is often thought to be applicable to mountaineering as a whole. It may have been the smart, quick answer to a tiresome questioner after a lecture, but it is not adequate. It does not bear examination. For as Donald Kinloch said, "It doesn't explain why mountaineers don't climb telegraph poles." But then, there has never really been a satisfactory explanation—satisfactory, that is, to mountaineer and layman alike.

As they rise massive from the earth's plain, soaring into the sky and sometimes hidden in cloud and mist, mountains are a challenge, a mystery, and another world. Men who climb mountains are, in their various ways, accepting this challenge to prove themselves against the peaks, as well as being enchanted by their essential mystery and beauty. The existence of the need or desire to prove or find one's self is, of course, well known and is the mainspring of most men's motives for climbing. Yet it does not explain fully what compels them to strive against weather, cold, and murderous physical discomfort in order to stand for a moment possibly without even a view to gratify them, on a cone of snow or pile of rocks which form a summit. There is another compulsion which comes, I believe, from the fascination surrounding the mystique of taking part in a struggle against odds, which absorbs every ounce of strength and nerve, yet for which there is no material reward. The attaining of the summit sets the seal on the selfless struggle. It is, if you like, a form of penance, or self-refinement; a sloughing off of all else to harden one's resolve and purpose into a shining point of sheer idealism.

Other motives do, of course, come into play. Mountains have been climbed in order to achieve fame, to gratify ambition, sometimes to uphold national pride and prestige, to glorify Teutonic prowess, or to complete a program of exploratory work. Or there may develop, in a man's mind, a personal relationship between himself and the mountain, as in the case of Whymper and the Matterhorn. But what attraction is it that draws men to the mountains and compels them to return again and again? It is because they are a different world and readily at hand. I have, on a winter's day, come through a freezing, killing blizzard on the summit of Snowdon, to arrive ninety minutes later in Llanberis to find mothers pushing their babies along the damp streets in open prams, in warm, almost muggy weather. They had no conception of this other world, two thousand feet above them, where storm and wind had raged in gripping cold in a desolation of rock. In time and space I had not traveled far, but in experience I had been to the other end of the earth.

Underlying all this is also the desire for adventure. Adventure is defined in the Oxford Dictionary as "a daring enterprise; an unexpected or exciting experience." The definition can be applied to any climb or mountain journey. Mountains are synonymous with adventure in the very nature of their remoteness, inaccessibility, and savagery of aspect.

There is also a revitalizing quality about the hills in their loneliness and beauty, in the ceaseless subtle interplay of cloud and light. It is no wonder that the ancient prophets took to the hills when beset by problems of the world. Call it escapism if you like, but what is wrong with that? There are still many men who find in the mountains a place to rediscover the truer and more lasting values of life.

Some of my own reasons for going to the mountains and the lonely places are succinctly stated by Thoreau: "I went to the woods because I wished to live deliberately, to front only the essential facts of life, and see if I could not learn what it had to teach, and not, when I came to die, discover that I had not lived."

What is often forgotten, in the search for inner meanings with an aura of mysticism, is that mountaineering is also a sport. A wide variety of knowledge and skills are required, which must be based on the essentials of physical toughness, nerve, judgment, and an understanding of men. The mountains themselves, and the ever present sense of danger, give to mountaineering that extra fascination and stature which physically and mentally make it one of the most enjoyable and rewarding of pastimes.

Then there is the wider scope of the enthralling business of planning expeditions and exploration. There are the pleasures of traveling in mountains with chosen companions and the fascinating study of one's fellow beings and the interaction of their emotions and characters under every sort of condition and environment. In the mountains a man's true worth is soon known. Under conditions of hardship when every man's work really matters and in the close proximity of living, the thin veneer which disguises many of our motives, emotions, and behavior in the outer world

is soon worn away. A man stands revealed for what he is,
and in this refining process a relationship of immense value
is often built up. When the struggle is for knowledge and
there is no material reward, that relationship will be pure
gold, and so will the men with whom one travels and climbs.

All this and more is summed up in the last few sentences
of Cherry Apsley Garrard's classic, *The Worst Journey in
the World,* when he writes: "If you have the desire for
knowledge and the power to give it physical expression, go
out and explore. If you are a brave man you will do nothing;
if you are fearful you may do much, for none but cowards
have need to prove their bravery. Some will tell you that
you are mad, and nearly all will say 'What is the use?' For
we are a nation of shopkeepers and no shopkeeper will look
at research which does not promise him a financial return
within a year. And you will sledge nearly alone, but those
with whom you sledge will not be shopkeepers; that is
worth a great deal."

A combination of these reasons had brought the four of
us into the mountains; had brought us to this untrodden col,
to lie, and wait, and hope, half buried in snow in the tiny
tent, our lives sustained only by its thin walls.

We made brew after brew of tea and hot lemonade. The
stove worked more efficiently after I had performed the delicate job of fitting a new nipple. Eating lunch whiled away
some more time, but we were bored and getting a trifle on
edge. Each time the stove was used a major reshuffle of bodies was required. The snow started, then stopped again, and
the prospect of making an ascent, or even moving far from
the tent, seemed unutterably remote.

Our morale fell and we talked of going down. We ate a
meager, uninteresting supper, for we were now on the special light rations, and for once even the thought of sleeping
did not appeal to anyone. Then suddenly Warwick started

to sing and we all joined in. We roared out song after song. Our spirits rose and we shouted defiance at the weather, the snow, and the threatening *séracs*. In turn we made our contributions. Our repertoire, acquired in Army and university, was extensive. We harmonized on French rounds, Swiss and German songs; we bawled out climbing ditties and parachuting ballads; songs fit to be heard in drawing rooms or only round a mess piano; songs about a certain O'Reilly's daughter; songs about the sad fate of a pugnacious lobster; a classic we called the "Traleika Cantata" which had no words at all, but only rude expressive noises; we ran through them one after the other. From the buried tent high up on this arctic col our voices rose in tuneless, but robust, unison.

At last it came to an end and we sat there, our throats dry and voices hoarse, just grinning at each other. I felt a great love and respect for these three bearded ruffians. I remembered that it was my wedding anniversary, and Warwick— proving equal to the occasion once more—drew from his trouser pocket a flask of whisky. The stove was produced and lemonade quickly brewed. We were soon sitting, almost luxuriously, sipping the hot toddy. In honor of the occasion we dubbed the east peak Anniversary Peak.

The snow had stopped by now and there was no wind; it was calm and still. One of Warwick's thermometers just outside the door showed the temperature to be near zero. The signs were good. Donald was firmly of the opinion that we would be able to climb tomorrow and, ever thoughtful of our welfare, doled out a ration of sleeping pills. I lay down in a happy mood and even decided that perhaps Warwick's feet did not smell too badly, and almost forgave Derek as he balled up again, driving his knees into my back.

14. *Anniversary Peak: The First Attempt*

MY MIND gradually swam to awareness, through the deep sublimity of sleep, towards the scuffling and noise of movement. A cold draft on my head made me open my eyes. Donald was just withdrawing his head from the entrance sleeve.

"The mist's clearing and it's beautifully still and cold, we ought to go," he whispered.

We woke the others and crammed back to the rear. Donald reached out, filled the billy from the stock of ice chips, and soon the blurred note of the Primus filled the tent.

After breakfast Warwick and I waited for the others to dress and quit the tent. Derek was out first and proclaimed in excited yells that it was "A perfect day." The yells continued, and Donald, answering in full cry, shot from the tent like a large ungainly projectile, scattering a pile of clothes Warwick had neatly collected on the floor and pushing him off balance into the side of the tent. Outside, still in process of dressing, Donald joined in the ecstatic chorus. We could hear him dancing with delight in the snow. Inside a disgruntled Warwick groveled for his scattered clothes and grumbled, "You clumsy monster Kinloch, when are you going to learn to live in a tent. I've now lost all my gloves."

This mundane and sordid concern, and the peevish reproval—in contrast to his own high state of excitement and impatience at our slowness—incensed Donald.

"You ——— phlegmatic Southern English!" he roared in fury.

There was only one answer to Donald when he was in this sort of mood, and that was to be even more phlegmatic. I took a great delight in saying firmly, "Now, now, doctor, you really must control yourself. These demonstrations are almost embarrassing."

The barb went home. With enormous contempt and sharp exasperation he volleyed back, "Oh, you inhibited English bastards."

We heard his grumbling to Derek. Inside the tent two Englishmen smiled at each other with complete understanding, then went on unhurriedly packing and dressing in a calm breakfast-time silence.

When we did emerge I understood Donald's joy. After days of enclosing mist the sight that met my eyes seemed almost unreal in its beauty. The sun circled in its low orbit, staining the peaks and snow around us with the delicate pink of its early rays. The air was frosted and crisp and came cleanly to the lungs like a revitalizing tonic after the vile, dead atmosphere of the tent. Against the deep, limitless blue of the sky the mountain tops stood out with gauzy clouds, like silk scarves draping their shoulders. The whole atmosphere was charged with a blueness which gave the effect of veil laid gently across the scene. Far away to the west I could see the rosy dome of McKinley rising grandly above its vast bulk, veiled with the powdery blue of the sky and garlanded with adorning vapors of cloud.

When we had left camp and turned the corner we saw Anniversary Peak close up for the first time. It presented to us a gigantic triangular face which rose in one vast, soaring, glistening sweep of snow to a corniced summit. The ridge, on which Warwick and I had climbed, swung round in a fantastic procession of cornices, gendarmes, and ice pitches to meet the nearest side of the triangle. Where it joined the face there was a notch eighty feet above the line of the bergschrund which marked the beginning of the face and the limit of the glacier. From this notch the face might be gained. The eye was drawn upwards from the notch and along the near side of the triangle from which cornices sprang to overhang, like a frieze, the southerly side. This grim, appalling precipice rose in a surging climax of rock and snow from the glacier beyond the col. Almost at the top of the triangle the direction of the cornices was reversed and they hung like fangs over the west face, forming a ridge which ran in waves to the summit.

At first sight I knew that there was no easy way to climb this mountain and there would be problems as yet unseen. The snow of the past few days would not have settled yet and would be prone to avalanches. This might prove the decisive factor. All that mattered was that we had accepted the challenge flung from the skies by this imperious peak, transfixing the azure like a barbed white arrowhead, and we were going forward to match it in the first glow of this glorious mountain day.

For some reason which I cannot explain, we began the climb in two separate parties, by different routes. Perhaps it was an unconscious reaction against the discipline and slowness of the four-man rope. The other two chose to traverse the ridge across the slopes of the col and then to climb the eighty-foot ice pitch which rose to the notch. Meanwhile Warwick and I made our way to the ridge. As we topped it a scene of beauty, even more breathtaking than that which lay behind, unfolded before us. This time our view was not confined to one glacier. We looked out beyond the head of the Ruth Glacier on an unexplored maze of broad ice highways which lapped the feet of countless snow-plastered rock peaks. This white wonderland sparkled and glistened in the sun, holding the eye, exerting an irresistible fascination. To the west, above a broad band of diaphanous cloud, floated the summit of Mount Foraker, its ice-fluted face impossibly high in the cerulean atmosphere. Far away the sky curved into the haze of distance and we thought we could just see the faint green of the Chulitna-Susitna valleys tingeing the harsher hues of the lower mountains. It was the most perfect mountain scene upon which I had ever set my eyes, and I stood there enraptured by its loveliness.

We at last turned away and started up the ridge. It was even more fearsome in clear weather than it had been in the mist. The cornices flung themselves out into space, and it was difficult to know at times whether we were on the ridge or not. Occasionally, we were very much aware that under our boot soles only a few inches of packed snow separated us from the aching void that hung below. The ice wall was quickly overcome, and moving fast we tight-roped daintily across the two saw-toothed knife-edges. We were moving well, our climbing full of understanding and anticipation for the others' safety and needs. We worked in almost perfect unison. Despite the danger inherent in climbing on such a ridge, I do not think I have enjoyed a climb more. Feelings of superb physical well-being, of absolute confidence in myself, and of complete trust in Warwick, combined to make these early hours on Anniversary Peak an unalloyed delight.

As we neared the notch, two cornices, upflung by wind, stood on the ridge about six feet apart, like two gendarmes. The only possible way past was on the lee side. Even so, on this side they bulged slightly, and the first steps had to be cut one-handed around the corner; next one had to make an airy move to occupy them. Forced out by the cornice, one needed delicate balance to stay in the tiny steps on the face of the ridge. I cut a finger hold and then with my left hand chipped the third step. Two more moves and I was sitting astride the ridge between the two cornices, belaying Warwick as he moved ahead to deal with the second.

The ridge then rose in an almost vertical fishtail about twenty feet high. We kicked steps up its ever narrowing flank, relying on our imbedded axe heads for a handhold. The exposure was impressive and we were not surprised to find as we gained the top that it was only just wide enough to take a boot. On both sides there was a sheer drop. But it was the Ruth Glacier side, falling away from the very edge of our boots for thousands of feet in violent, plunging lines of ice and rock, which for a moment filled me with its awfulness. It was no place to linger.

A long section of cornice followed, and I belayed Warwick from what I thought was a safe place. When he was halfway across, the snow beneath me dropped a few inches with a dull crumping noise. My heart stopped. I knew that I was on the cornice. I heard a rumbling and saw snow cascading down the precipice below. Part of the underneath had gone. I had a frightening vision of my own body following it in a hissing cloud of snow.

We've pushed our luck too far. The thought seared across my mind. "Get moving. This whole lot's going," I gasped at Warwick, who stood startled and transfixed. In a few strides he was on the notch, his axe in and the rope round it. There was an eternity while he took in the slack and then, "Come on."

I remembered only arriving on the notch and that we were both trembling. Looking back I saw that the cornice was still there, looking thick and solid. "Very dodgy," I said, "I thought we were going to get down to the Ruth Glacier after all." The others were still only two-thirds of the way up the ice, well below the notch. We looked down on the tops of their heads and saw the line of the ice falling sheer from their feet. It was very steep.

Huge cornices overhung the notch and there was no way directly onto the face. I therefore began to kick steps up the steep slope behind, which rose under the cornices like a ramp and seemed to run parallel with the angle of the face. After fifty feet it came to an end, and a traverse across the steep wall beneath the cornices began. I could not yet see whether this course would enable me to get to a point where I could break through the cornices onto the west face, but I was hopeful.

Shouts from Warwick below told me that the others had arrived on the notch. While they were joining onto our rope I hammered a piton into the ice, which was now exposed just above me. I clipped myself to this, and thus safe-guarded, cut a wide ice ledge to make a safe stance from which I could bring the others up. It was hard work. The sun was already around and glinting on the ice-furred un-dersides of the cornices above me. Warwick came up and instantly rejected the idea of the traverse.

"If you could give me a shoulder I might be able to scramble up through this cornice above," he suggested.

"I could never hold you. Donald will have to come up to give a hand."

Luckily the ledge was large enough for the three of us. Donald secured himself with another piton and we tried to push Warwick up. But it was no good; the cornices were too far above us, and there was the danger of a piece being dislodged by Warwick which might knock us from our stance. Firmly belayed by Warwick, I ventured out on the traverse. The snow was soft, and on my third step a sheet of it beneath my foot buckled and slid away, launching it-self into three thousand feet of space in a disintegrating cloud. For a moment I was left balancing on one foot; then I retreated to the ice platform.

"It's no good, Jimmy," said Donald. "It's too late in the day. This snow will avalanche if you even look at it."

An unseen jet aircraft bored its way through the sky and the very air seemed to quiver. We all looked upwards instinctively, as if expecting the vibrating waves to shatter the predatory cornices above, bringing them smashing down on us. Regretfully, Warwick and I agreed with Donald, and we returned carefully one by one to the waiting Derek on the notch. At Warwick's suggestion we drove in a piton above the ice pitch and abseiled down. We left the rope fixed there to aid our return the next day.

When we reached the camp Derek complained of sickness and seemed on the verge of collapse. His grey face looked ghastly, for it was mottled with blood and his lips were bleeding. Donald was somewhat puzzled until Derek explained that while climbing the ice pitch he had placed a piton in his mouth in order to free his hands. The cold metal had immediately frozen to his lips, and in hurriedly removing it he had stripped the skin from them. His tongue was also blistered. He was an unhappy sight. Donald gave Derek the inevitable pill; upon swallowing it he collapsed unconscious into the snow. We were amazed. Warwick exclaimed, with rather uncertain humor, "You've done it this time, doctor, you really have fixed him. I told you those pills were cripplers."

I assisted the perplexed Donald in hauling Derek to his feet. As soon as he was upright he came to life and said, "Where am I?"

Warwick, who by now thought it was some sort of act, said scornfully, "Battersea Dogs' Home" (Derek lived opposite in a trailer).

This remark seemed to revive Derek. At least, he called

Warwick a most uncharitable name, so Donald and I released him, whereupon he fell down again.

It all seemed rather queer to me but Donald, muttering curious terms, was professionally concerned and seemed to be making some sort of diagnosis. We picked up Derek and sat him down. His woolen hat had fallen over one eye and he looked like a drunken doll. He sat there looking dazed until hot tea revived him. Warwick continued to be unimpressed and diagnosed it as a "monster Pritchard trick." It was true that Derek could be a little fanciful and was rather Walter Mitty-like, but we never did discover the reasons for his behavior.

By now it was misting over and the keen wind drove us into the tent. I was confident of good weather that night, and we fell asleep vowing to finish off the peak on the next attempt.

15. *Defeat on Anniversary Peak*

THE ALARM failed us and we made a late start, but by five o'clock we were on the notch. It was another glorious day and despite the sun, the temperature was around zero Fahrenheit. From the ice stance above the notch I moved out onto the traverse. I was determined to climb the peak that day. The mountain had become a personal challenge to me. For some reason—which I did not fully understand myself—its ascent seemed to be a fitting tribute to my wife, possibly because of its association with our wedding anniversary.

The snow was slightly firmer, but still not safe, and as I made the first step I knew that this part at any rate was going to be dangerous. Warwick was number two and then came the others. We were all tied together on two 125-foot ropes. I moved slowly, my crampons sinking in a few inches with each step. Each time, I gradually transferred my weight from one foot to the next, never relying on a new step until it felt absolutely firm. In places the snow was quite hard, but underneath there was ice into which my crampon spikes bit. This gave me a false assurance, for it was also a perfect gliding surface on which the new snow could avalanche. Above, the dreadful cornices like deathly white talons hung over my path. I balanced upright, out away from the angle of the snow axe held in front across my body, my right hand on the head, the left grasping the shaft, with the point just touching the snow, ready to be brought into action should I slip. Foot by foot I advanced, feeling the ever increasing pull of the rope on my chest as the distance between Warwick and myself increased. At fifty feet I knew that if I fell there would be little chance of Warwick's holding me. Here I cleared away the snow at about waist height, exposing a layer of rotten ice. After more digging I came to hard ice and drove a piton in. To this I attached a snap-link and passed my rope through. Thus protected, I moved on.

The angle steepened and the snow was deeper. It was no longer safe to move sideways and so I turned inwards to face the snow. Raising my axe I drove it in hard. It sank in and was held rock-steady by the enclosing snow. *Good; this was going to be slow and tricky work. Out with the right foot. Get in.* I drove my toe in and down, three times; on the third kick it rested instep-deep and felt secure. *Weight on the right foot. Now kick in the left. Three more kicks and in. Out and in with the axe. Two feet to the right this time. Now right foot again. Left into the waiting pigeonhole and so on.*

The sweat tingled on my skin and I felt the dampness of the wool around my forehead. I was intensely alive and ultrasensitive to everything around me. My ears and eyes were alert for any warning or noise of snow movement which might precede a breaking step, or avalanche, or cornice fall. My mind, controlling nerves strung for quick response, was clear and calm, answering the problems easily, directing the body pinned to the snow, delicately balanced between substance and space. This solitary struggle which made the ultimate demands on mind, nerve, and muscle filled me with a fierce unquenchable joy. In these moments

I possessed myself utterly; holding cupped in the palm of my endeavor, my own tiny spark of life, wagering it against the challenge of the mountain.

I could pick out every crystal of snow on the surface a few inches in front of my face. The gleam of the blade, and the soft whiteness of the shaft, smoothed and scored by countless thrusts through snow, etched themselves on my mind. *How was this snow sticking on? Perhaps because it was confined by the ice ribs, just ahead, running down from the cornice. Not far now, and I might be able to see a way through above onto the face.* I drove in the axe. There was a shock which ran up the shaft, numbing my hands as the point was rejected by hard ice. For a moment I was off balance, arching back over the drop. Then fear springing inside me electrified my reaction. I struck back, bringing down the pick of the axe viciously through the snow into the ice beneath. I held on, feeling the pull of the void, falling away beneath my feet, gradually growing less. As I hung there waiting for my breathing and my heartbeats to slow down, a doubt about going on flickered across my mind and was thrust out. I whistled softly as I began to move once more. Beyond the rib there was nothing.

"Warwick," I called back, "I can't get on on this line. I'll move up towards the cornices." My voice sounded unnaturally high and slightly unsteady as it cut the silence.

"O.K., but take it steady. I nearly had a fit just now when I thought you were coming off."

The snow had piled up against the rib deep and compact. Using the lower part of my leg only, I drove my foot in three, four, five times to make each step, and slowly climbed away from the jutting eave of snow below. The rib fused with the cornice on its underside and presented a ten-foot ice wall. I cut a platform at its base, then two steps above it, and then two more nicks above them. I intended to overcome the wall by sheer speed and force. Up into the first two steps . . . in with the axe pick just below the top . . . a pull on the axe . . . crampon points into the upper nicks . . . an arm over the top . . . a slip which robbed me for a split second of my upward momentum . . . a push on the axe head and I was up, sitting astride the wall. Beyond, another couloir and a rib, and above . . . oh wonderful! . . . a mere lip of a cornice—and the sky.

"I think it'll go," I called to the unseen Warwick. "Another hundred feet or so, and I can get onto the face."

"Good-oh!" he shouted back. "Can I come up?"

"Yes, up to the piton first, and I'll protect you from here."

I heard him relay my words to the others and I thought I caught the sound of an ironic cheer. They had been waiting a long time. I drove my axe deeply into a crack in the top of the wall and took a turn of the rope around it.

"Come on, Warwick."

The rope slackened. I began to take it in and soon Warwick appeared, moving steadily. I watched him carefully, my knees gripping the wall. From above, the route looked spectacular. It appeared as a frail necklace of blemishes in the purity of the snow which roofed the thrusting wall of rock and ice rising from the glacier. The puny marks of man's techniques, defying Nature and the pulling power of the void below. At the piton Warwick cut himself a secure stance and snapped a loop through the karabiner, securing himself. Another eighty feet or more down the rope I knew that Donald, on the first ice platform, would be also protecting Warwick. I felt comforted by the thought of the teamwork and mutual confidence which linked us across the snow. The solitary feeling I had out in front was in my mind only and not a thing of fact.

"Right, Warwick, I'll move just down to the other side of the wall and belay you from there," I called. "You can all move up then."

He nodded. I withdrew my axe and the rope tightened on my chest. I slid off the wall and let myself down the other side, using the axe shaft—hanging from its indriven pick—as a hand rail. When I was in position I called for the others to move. I stood there thinking about the filming, wishing that we could record this climb. But it was unlikely that Derek would be able to take any pictures. Just when the scenery was at its best and the combination of snow, ice, rock, space, and climbing was at its most spectacular he would be debarred from filling it by the demands of safety. My thoughts were broken by a shout from Warwick and again I took in his rope, the nylon purring softly against the wood, until it lay in a long loop below me. Then the thud of boots, and a scuffling noise; the rib seemed to shake and Warwick's face came in sight topped by his absurd white woolen hat.

When he was firmly astride he said, "What a monster route, Mills. Donald was ticking like a clock at the wait. Since he started on the traverse he's a lot quieter. But don't slip again. I'd have been pushed to hold you last time, but we're a bit more secure now."

The crossing to the rib was a slightly steeper repetition of the first traverse—the enormous drop, the occasional pitches of ice where I cut steps, the steady progress on flexed ankles, a piton in the middle, a life depending on twenty steel crampon points. I based myself on some flakes of rock which marked the end of the rib and the top of the great precipitous wall which fell to the glacier. Secured by my axe, I looked back along the looping rope which brushed the pockmarks of my steps, to where Warwick sat astride the wall intent on the progress of the other two. There was a long wait ahead, and before me stretched the glorious pageant of mountain, glacier, and sky. I took some photographs —probably an unjustified act at the time, but later they became a vital part of the pictorial history of the expedition. The sun slowly moved in the sky, and the deep silence was occasionally broken by the clatter and whirr of stones freed from the ice below me by the heat.

At last the long process of movement of rope and men brought Warwick moving towards me and soon he stood by my side on the rib.

"I'm going straight up on the far side of this rib," I told him, "and I'm going as fast as I can."

After the first few steps upward I found the snow and ice were rotten, and the angle much steeper than I had thought. Each step crumbled if my weight was in it for more than a second or two, producing a heart-stopping slip. There was a good fifty feet to go at an unrelenting angle. To clear away the rotten surface and cut steps in the hard ice underneath would take hours. It was a case of going up and fast, or going down. I moved upwards. Warwick later described it as "swimming up to the cornices." My weight barely settled on either foot before I stepped up again. For handholds I punched my left fist in hard and used the axe head in my right hand as a claw. I drove myself up and up. To stop would be to fall. Sheer speed and movement kept me attached, by some attraction, to the face. I knew nothing except that I must go on. The small ceaseless gentle movements drew the flaw in the cornices nearer and nearer. I climbed almost possessed, my mind goading me on, barricading my taut nerves against fear. I muttered as I strove upwards. "It must go . . . I must stay on"—the chant bubbled over my lips. I willed the snow and ice to hold me. My head broke through the embryo cornices and the snow sprayed over me. I looked across the vast, stark, slanting expanse. Another surge upwards and I was able to drive the shaft of my axe a few inches into the face and hold on. Out of the trance I heard my breath rasping and the convulsive pounding of my heart. I was up! I was safe . . . !

With my free hand I flogged away the cornice and then heaved myself up. The face was so steep I found it difficult to get my crampons in. When I did, I stood upright and swiftly cut a broad ledge in the ice just beneath the snow. Standing on this I drove in a piton. Secure myself, I put my axe back in the hole I had first made, belayed Warwick, and shouted, "I'm up!" It sounded like a cry of triumph from *Excelsior*. I suddenly felt terribly lonely on this tilted snow desert.

I saw Donald move doggedly across below, then Warwick started up. He moved fast. All space seemed to draw him down. I kept the rope tight.

"Keep moving," I shouted, desperate for him to stay on. It was difficult to see the steps from above. An enormous relief drained through me as he struggled onto the minute platform. The strain was etched into the lineaments of his features. "What a bastard," he said.

He turned to bring Donald up and I began to extend the platform. Finding the loop connecting me to the piton was too short to allow me to work properly, I exchanged it for another. As I did this I automatically checked the security of the piton. It came out in my hands. With a startled cry I lurched teetering backwards. Warwick, in the act of protecting Donald, turned and flung out an arm; his fingers hooked in my chest harness. Off balance, we rocked outwards. My eyes, focused down Warwick's crooked fingers and rigid arm, looked into his widening eyes. Momentarily we were poised over space locked together. Then slowly we overcame the outward pull and recovered.

"Thanks, Warwick, sorry about that." It sounded fatuous. I grinned weakly.

"For God's sake make sure the thing's in properly this time," he snapped back.

I knocked in two pitons, one each. Donald came up complaining about the weight of Derek's camera which he was carrying. In a short time Derek joined us, crowding the tiny ledge; it was only about six inches wide and three feet long. I asked Derek to lead on. There was a stretch of ice ahead and he was probably the fastest step-cutter. After a short pause he started up moving daintily, economical with his axe strokes. The ice chips began to fly and scud past us.

The broad white expanse swept up and up, corrugated with tiny waves. Warwick estimated the angle at about sixty degrees; it may have been more—it was very steep. Fringing the top and overhanging the face were the enormous icicle-bearded cornices we had seen from below. Derek aimed at the point where they started. From here we hoped to follow the ridge to the summit.

Above the ice, about fifty feet up, Derek came onto firm snow. The others gradually moved up one by one, but it seemed an age before I was called forward by Warwick to the first stance. So we continued from belay to belay, Derek up fifty feet or so; then I moved; Donald up to Warwick; Warwick to Donald; Donald to Derek. Then the process began again. The snow grew softer and climbing became more laborious as we ploughed a furrow up the face. The long line of rope looped and stretched upwards, then looped again.

Derek heard it first: the low murmur of an aircraft engine from out of the north.

"Listen, it's a plane."

We stood stock still in our pits in the snow, straining our

ears. The hum grew louder. Then we saw it circling Tatum and Waggoner's Col. After a while the great four-engined transport veered away and came on up the glacier. Derek began to wave. We all waved. The elongated shadows of our arms semaphored across the face. Suddenly the aircraft changed course and came straight at us. I was delighted. Somehow the pilot had seen us. The anxiety about possible rescue attempts was over. Twice he flew by, and as he made the third turn we could see that he was coming even closer to the peak.

"He's going to make a drop," I shouted.

"I hope he doesn't come too close or he'll have those cornices down on us," said Warwick, always the practical climber.

The great machine came slowly closer, now at our height, throttling back and crabbing slightly across the sky. As it drew opposite, its long smooth fuselage glinting in the sun, one of the two figures in the door threw something out. It fell, a small dark package trailing an orange streamer. The two men in the doorway waved back and the plane throbbed by over the col, the propeller blades silver discs of light in the misty blue air. Our eyes followed the streamers down the thousands of feet to our tracks which led from the camp, and it appeared to land right on them. It was a superb exhibition of flying and air dropping. We wondered what was in the package—mail, or just a message? Our eyes turned back and upwards to the cornices above. We moved on towards them.

Derek was tiring, his movements hampered by the snow. In the rear Warwick and I found the climbing easy and a little tedious. Climbing continuously on the steep face, Derek turned the cornice and stood on top. We waited hopefully for his decision. He bawled back, "It's no good. Too dicey . . . Double cornices all the way and the summit's a long way off." Unconvinced, Donald moved up beside him, but reported the same finding.

I said to Warwick, "I'm sure it'll go. It won't be any worse than the first ridge to the notch."

We had almost decided to go up when Donald returned and said, "It's not worth it; we'd better stick to the face."

Above us there was a low crump. Our heads jerked upwards. Derek reappeared, moving very fast, and positively shot down to where we stood.

"The whole lot dropped under me. I've had that ridge in a big way now." He looked very shaken.

I took the lead again and traversed left and upwards towards the summit cornices. Our tracks made a parapet across the snow. I began to sink into the powdery snow up to my thighs. Sometimes I could not touch bottom and floundered like a learner at his first swimming lesson. At others my crampons pressed into ice. Overhead, the cornices threatened our very existence, and occasionally icicles broke off and slithered down the face. I was scarcely making any progress upwards. As far as I could judge, two hundred feet of high-angled snow separated us from the top. It was late in the day; the sun glared full on the face. How was the snow staying on at this angle? The question worried and nagged at me.

The summit seemed tantalizingly near; it was difficult to acknowledge what I knew to be good mountaineering sense. We were strung out on a face which might avalanche at any moment, under murderous cornices with scarcely a good belay between us. The rest of the slope was even steeper, and in these conditions it could take us hours to reach the top.

I looked back at the others standing on the parapet of snow, pinned to the face with their ice axes, waiting for my next move. They looked tired and without enthusiasm. I

looked up across the glittering snow and thought of all the
waiting days; the two previous attempts; the desperate
struggle to gain the face; and the fact that this would be our
last chance. I wanted to go on; to climb this mountain. I
knew also that my own selfish desire had brought us—by
scarcely justifiable climbing—to this danger point.

"We've got to make a decision now. I'd like to go on.
What do you think?" I asked them.

Warwick, standing next to me, said, "All right, I'll have
a go."

His voice was dull and there was no keenness, but I knew
that he would go on.

"You see our track," said Donald, jerking his head downwards, "it reminds me of the perforations between stamps
—ready to tear off at any moment."

He was right.

"A lot of people didn't believe that picture, in the Everest
book, of the Sherpa on the Lhotse face. They'd believe it if
they saw us here," said Derek, talking in some sort of par-
able.

No one would really say a definite "Yes" or "No." The
decision was mine. We must go down. It was over, then.

"All right, we'll go down. Push on, Derek."

We moved back to meet the upcoming tracks, and Warwick led down. Rope length after rope length we climbed
down, one at a time. On the ice platform I asked Warwick,
as he was leading, to abseil down far enough to be able to
drop through the cornices onto the stance above the notch.
It was a rather desperate way of getting down, but it was
safer than retracing our steps under the whole length of the
cornices, and quicker. The rest of us unclipped from the
rope and it was passed through the piton we had used on
the ascent. Warwick started off, sidling down the face, then
passed from view around the bulge of a cornice. The rope

tightened, grew slack, then snapped tight again. Unknown to us he had crashed through a cornice, finding himself rather higher up than planned. Derek followed, and again there was an enormous jerk transmitted up the rope to the piton where Donald and I stood. He had also gone down through the cornices with a rush, almost knocking Warwick from his precarious perch.

I saw Donald disappear out of sight and was left by myself on the face. It was an awful, lonely place. The mist swirled around me, blown by a sharp, cold wind. I had been standing on the six-inch platform for over an hour and my feet were beginning to freeze. At last the slackening of the rope told me that I could go down. I took a last hopeful look at the piton and abseiled off the ledge and through the cornices to join Donald again. He was more tired than I had ever seen him, and anxious to be off the mountain. Thankfully the rope came easily from the piton without bringing too much of the cornice down on us.

The others had put up a fixed rope as a handrail which made the climb down to the notch considerably safer. I again abseiled down last, from the ice pitch, and we plodded down the channel of our track back to camp, picking up the package of mail on the way. We had been away fifteen hours, and supper, even on half rations, was very welcome.

The defeat rankled at my mind. I accused myself of lack of courage and determination and of bad judgment. I tried to rationalize the final decision as good mountaineering sense, but it did not satisfy my ego or soften the disappointment.

Often in mountains, in these circumstances, the lurking, half-sensed motivating force behind this sort of decision is fear; and it is difficult to bring oneself to recognize fear and to admit that one is afraid. Sometimes the mind-crippling

emotion is nervously swamped in bravado, and an unjustified attempt is pursued. Or fear is called by some other
name, like "mountaineering judgment"—to satisfy the con-
science—and defeat is accepted. Yet even so, the decisive
factor on Anniversary Peak had been the bad and dangerous snow conditions brought about by the prolonged bliz-
zards of the past week. The late start had also robbed us of
vital time.

While the Primus purred softly under a last brew of hot
lemonade I drew some consolation from the letters from
home.

16. Return to the Glacier

WE FOUND a thick mist engulfing the tent when we awoke, and there was snow in the wind. We were all tired and moved slowly; dressing and packing took a long time. For breakfast there were only a few scraps, and the sole remaining food was our 24-hour emergency pack. We had pushed home the attempt on Anniversary Peak to the very last and now we had to get down whatever the conditions.

The tent was completely frozen in, and it was necessary to chip the floor-cloth from our bed of ice. Shoveling the snow away was exhausting work. With only one shovel, we took it in turns. In the intervals we listlessly collected our loads together, fumbling with straps, the metal of the frames burning our fingers. I took my gloves off and put them on again a score of times.

When the tent was folded and the bulky loads strapped to the frames, Donald suggested a step test. Understandably enough, no one was very keen. I knew that Donald had planned on this as part of his program, so self-righteously, feeling a true martyr to science, and at the same time trying to shame the others, I volunteered. It was exhausting, but in the end everyone did his stint.

Feeling a little the worse for wear we set out that afternoon at four-thirty, and I led down into the gloom. I could see nothing ahead, but in the rear, compasses in hand, the others directed my course. On the steep slopes the snow was like liquid, flowing past us in small slides. At intervals we were forced to stop when the snow, building up behind, threatened to sweep us forward with it. In the mist, with unseen danger all around, a sense of doom pressed upon us and we moved fearfully. Several times I pulled up on the very edges of crevasses which had suddenly come into focus in the murk. For some time we veered this way and that, losing faith in our sense of direction and our compasses, until a *sérac* loomed up before us and was recognized as the point reached on our early reconnaissance from Banana *Sérac* Camp. We turned the corner and came onto the broader snow slopes.

The others were tired, and from the rear irritated shouts told me to slow down. The effect of short rations was most marked in Warwick, the biggest man. I thought it would be best if he made his own pace in front and we reversed the lead.

A clearing in the mist gave Warwick a view of what he thought was a roadway through the *séracs* leading down to the glacier. Remembering the danger of avalanche on our original route, we decided, after some argument, in favor of Warwick's half-seen path. After a few hundred yards Warwick recoiled from the brink of an ice cliff and we knew that we were among the great area of riven blocks. Mist and snow formed a single wall in front; we could distinguish nothing ahead, nor could we tell if our next step would be onto snow or thin air.

Warwick, in front, was in constant danger of stepping over one of the enormous cliffs and we kept him on a tight rope. He began throwing a route flag a few yards ahead. If he could still see it when it landed, he knew he could go on safely. His ingenuity did not end there. When he found the flag-throwing too arduous he rolled black currant pastilles ahead. It was like cocking a snook at the mountains. So we went on almost lightheartedly, following the route as it opened up before us. The mist maintained our blissful ignorance of the risks we ran and at last, after leaving a large gully, we came onto the glacier, almost tripping over one of our route flags. There was no doubt that luck was with us that night.

I was so convinced of this that in spite of the treacherous, concealing snow I told the others I had a hunch no one would go through. I felt extremely happy and fit and rather contemptuous of my wan, foot-dragging companions. In this carefree mood I was moved to break into song, my voice echoing bizzarely in the murky canyon. The others bore my dreadful heartiness well. Fifty yards further on, after my cheerful prophecy, Derek went down to his waist.

We found the forlorn tent of Terminus Camp almost flattened by snow. Here we took our first rest and brewed tea. After striking the tent we loaded the sledge and pulled on into the grey silence, the sledge wallowing and sinking deeply into the white morass. There were frequent halts during which the leader probed for crevasses, and after each pause we found that the sledge had settled down and was stuck fast. It required all our concerted strength, as time and time again we flung ourselves forward, to move the sledge. I began to feel sick from the savage jerking of the harness against my stomach.

Derek's snowshoes and mine gave way under the strain. Without them we moved painfully slowly, plunging and floundering our way forward, exhaustion sapping our efforts. Near Raven's Camp I had the unnerving experience of breaking through into crevasses—probably the same one —five times in twenty yards. My friends, gentlemen that that they are, refrained from saying "We told you so."

Manhauling in these conditions, with a heavy sledge, was obviously too dangerous, so leaving it in a safe and obvious place we went forward to reconnoiter with light loads on our backs.

After meandering for endless minutes in sight of the camp Donald eventually led us through safely. The tent was almost down and the floor running with icy water. Derek feared for his film, left behind in a box, but fortunately all the reels were untouched. We returned safely to the lightened sledge and quickly made the final lap into camp. It was three-thirty that morning when we thankfully threw down the traces.

After the two tents were put up we would have collapsed into our sleeping bags without food, but Warwick, with heroic patience and strength of mind, cooked a wonderfully tasty curry. That one thoughtful act earned him my deeper admiration.

The sun drove use from our clammy sleeping bags after barely six hours of unsatisfactory sleep. We were all still tired, and very irritable. The weeks of load-carrying, lack of sleep, and the nervous strain were beginning to tell on us. Derek and Warwick seemed to be the most tired and their nerviness was more obvious. All of us were suffering from snow blindness, Derek and Donald quite badly. Donald diagnosed his as eyestrain caused by the difficulty of seeing my steps, on the traverse below the lower cornices on Anniversary Peak.

For the rest of the morning we reorganized the food and equipment and busied ourselves with a succession of domestic chores and the hateful snowshoe repair. Our beards had improved considerably, and lately we had taken to admiring them in the carefully preserved remains of a mirror —excepting Donald, who had brought a clockwork razor with him and had maintained an almost suave smoothness. His reason for shaving was purely commercial. With the aid of some well-posed photographs and what he termed "an unsolicited testimonial," he hoped to recoup some of his outlay on the expedition from the razor manufacturers. Unfortunately, all he received for his trouble was a polite letter of thanks.

The day was warm and clear and we could look back at Charybdis Col peaceful and unclouded in the sun. Across the face of Anniversary Peak were the tracks of avalanches, their debris spreading fanlike across the slopes below the col. It was blissful to wander about in the sun after the days of confining storm and mist. Derek, ever proud of his physique and manhood, and impervious to the sun, wore only his boots and a small revealing towel. More discreetly I favored an old blue shirt and pajama trousers tucked into my boot tops. The tents were festooned with sleeping bags and clothing. Lines rigged between ice axes carried an equally colorful assortment.

At mid-morning, when we broke off work for a cup of coffee, the well-worn subject, which I facetiously called the "Great Alpine Controversy," was resurrected by Donald. He insisted that everything we did in the mountains should be governed by the principles established over the years of Alpine experience. I argued that although most of the basic rules still applied as in the Alps, nonetheless in Alaska, where the mountains, weather, and snow conditions differed they did not all have the same force. Furthermore, on an expedition some risks were necessarily taken, perhaps even forced upon climbers, which would be quite unjustifiable on an Alpine holiday. Derek and Warwick took sides and fed the fire of controversy. I could see that Donald had not been at all happy about the conduct of the Anniversary Peak attempt. Unfortunately, in my heated defense, I brought the argument down to a personal level and charged him with undue caution. Donald did not see himself at all in this light and reacted violently. The argument ended abruptly with sharp angry words, and there was an uncomfortable, resentful atmosphere in the camp for some time.

These clashes are almost inevitable in any expedition. Especially in times of stress and fatigue, when tempers and feelings are near the surface, collisions of mood and temperament are certain to occur. They themselves are of no great moment, but what is important is that ill feeling and resentment should not be borne secretly. In time they will poison the whole spirit of the party and weaken its purpose. The suppression of these feelings is impossible for long and they explode with far worse effects later. In a small expedition like ours, whose strength depends absolutely on the closest cooperation and complete confidence between all the members, this corroding atmosphere must be avoided at all costs. For it will eat away at the soul of the party until nothing remains of morale, friendship, and confidence. The bright endeavor, so optimistically embarked upon, will be a ruin. A timely apology after a clash is the only answer. It calls for a good deal of selflessness and good will, but it is worth it.

Over lunch good relationships were resumed, and hard words forgotten, when Donald introduced us to Rank Bajin and Lobey Dosser, the principal characters of a strip cartoon in one of the Glasgow newspapers. It is a product of Scottish whimsy which appealed even to us—the English —after Donald's narrative in the vernacular, so much so that we dropped the inappropriate title of doctor and called him Rank. I think he was quite pleased.

When the work was completed we amused ourselves by drafting a mock script and shooting sequence for an advertising film. It was the saga of an expedition which was failing in its attempts on a peak, because of tiredness and lack

of resolution on the part of one of its key members. How
the climber is introduced by one of the members to a famous bedtime drink, which makes a new man of him and
assures the expedition's success, makes—as the blurbs say
—a fitting climax to the story.

Says the leader, at Base Camp after the successful ascent,
"Without that carry of Fred's to the col we could never have
climbed Dhaurlic."

Closeup of Fred's profile against mountain and sky,
thinks "Thanks to. . . ."

Amid all the fooling we took some still shots of happy
mountaineers imbibing the famous beverages. The sequel
to this came when we asked the War Office if we might be
allowed to approach the manufacturers with the proposal
that the photographs could be used as advertising material.
We hoped to get a substantial reward for our talented efforts. Unfortunately the public relations experts at Whitehall crushed our hopes with a well-considered ruling. The
photographs might only be used, they said, if we were
shown as being in uniform and clean-shaven. Officers displaying themselves in mufti, with beards! Gad, what next!

In the evening we discussed final plans for the last phase
of the expedition. It was now the twenty-eighth of June, and
allowing a minimum of two and a half days to get out to
meet the helicopter, at noon on July 7, we had only six clear
days in which to finish off our program. To complete our
scheme of scientific and exploratory work we had still to
make a journey up the right fork of the glacier, an attempt
on Pegasus Peak and if possible Koven or Carpe. Donald's
medical program and Warwick's meteorological record were
progressing according to plan and only required pushing
on to their normal completion.

Derek's filming was in the same state and he had made
virtually a complete record of the expedition. In so doing

he had exposed himself not only to considerable danger on innumerable occasions, but also to the wrath and abuse of us all. No one when he is tired likes retracing exhausting steps, or when in a hurry being delayed "just to get this shot right." The fact that at most times he managed to achieve some sort of cooperation from us was eloquent of his persuasiveness and tact. We had acquired enough data to report on rations and equipment, and I needed only one journey to the other side of the glacier to complete the geological survey.

We decided, therefore, to spend the next day adding to the geological collection, filming, and carrying out final tests for Donald. The following two or three days were to be devoted to a journey up the fork, from which an attempt at Koven or Carpe might result. Then, finally, an attempt on Pegasus, and withdraw. It was an optimistic plan and did not allow for delays.

The evening meal was almost a feast. Derek scraped together the remains of our luxury box into a four-course meal and also produced a menu in fine script, which read:

Soup au Traleika
Curry a la De Coque
Peche Crevasse
Doigts des Singes

There were also biscuits, cheese, whisky toddy, and Ovaltine.

After the meal we lolled back on our sleeping bags savoring the bouquet of the whisky, like gourmets. We talked not so much of the final week in the mountains, but of what we were going to do in Canada, on the boat, and in England. It was obvious that we had all nearly had enough. The conversation droned on pleasantly until we became conscious of the fact that the curry—to which Warwick had

given his name—was manifesting itself in the usual un-
pleasant manner. On these occasions our discomfort and
complaints had the effect of reducing Warwick to helpless
laughter. As always, we were forced to quit the tent leaving him, incontinent and hysterical, on the floor. Later, I
described the incident as I thought Robert Service might
have put it in one of his sagas.

Theirs was the shock when the grinning Deacock,
Gave vent to vapors obscene.
In the Meade that night aghast at their plight,
Sat the men whose friend he had been.
Past hardships they'd shared were as nothing compared,
To this foul, insidious, blight.
With oaths deeply meant they burst from the tent,
Out in the pure Arctic night.
It was twenty below as they stood in the snow,
Frostbitten by a wind that was keen.
Though their limbs might freeze black there was no going back,
In there where the air had turned green.

The next morning the journey to the other side of the
glacier was fairly successful, in spite of enormous *séracs* and
the bergschrund. We returned with a number of useful specimens.

Before lunch we attempted to inject some more excitement into the film by filming a mock fall into a crevasse, and
the subsequent rescue. As the victim, I disappeared from
the camera's view by dropping onto a ledge, some six feet
below the surface, in a large crevasse. Unfortunately, because of the overhang and trouble with my prusik loops, it
developed into a rather uncomfortable experience involving a proper rescue, and we were taught a salutory lesson
not to meddle with crevasses.

During lunch we were surprised by the appearance of the
C-54 over Charybdis Col. By lighting flares we attracted it

down the glacier, where it made slow circuits at a considerable height above the camp. Now that we could see each other, and the wireless was at hand, it was worth one more attempt at radio contact.

I spoke into the set. "British mountaineering party calling. Our wireless damaged. Believe we can send, but not receive. If you can hear me, please wiggle your wings." It was like inviting a stately dowager to rhumba. There was a slow, dignified roll of the fuselage and the sun flashed on the great wings. That was all we wanted to know.

"Nothing heard, but your signal seen. Will meet helicopter Cache Creek at noon July 7." The aircraft banked again in answer, as it rode in its leisurely orbit.

"That's all," I said. "Goodbye."

Early in the afternoon, after carrying out more tests for Donald, we packed up for the next journey. It seemed to take a long time. There were endless things to be done and more tedious snowshoe repairs. As we saw the work eating into our valuable sleeping time there were fresh bursts of annoyance. By the time we finally got down to sleep there had been several bitter rows, apologies, and counterapologies, until we were not, any of us, on speaking terms.

17. Reconnaissance

WE DID NOT sleep well that night, and morale sank even lower when on awaking we found a clammy pall of mist around us. After an hour of argument I managed to convince a tired Derek, and a sceptical Donald, that it was worth making a start. When we did pull away I began to doubt my own judgment. The snow was soggy and the mist made crevasses invisible, reducing our march to a crawl. Derek gave up the lead, after only a few hundred yards, complaining that he could see nothing and that it was too dangerous to continue. Warwick took over and we crept on through the silent, yellow murk. It was necessary to probe every inch of the way, and for all of us it was a nerve-straining, temper-fraying journey. Donald, in spite of Warwick's cautious and safe leading, would insist on rechecking every inch of the way, which slowed us up even more.

Shortly after I had taken over, the glacier surface became more uneven. Ice hummocks and small *séracs* made the sledge-hauling a greater drudgery, but Donld will persisted in his double-checking until I could bear it no longer.

"Donald, if you feel that you can't trust the leader then you should have stayed in camp. I can't bear it when you're scratching about behind me like an old hen."

"I'm just making sure," said Donald doggedly.

When his turn came the mist had cleared slightly. He began racing forward, throwing caution to the winds, as if to show, after his display of hesitance, what a tiger he really was. The pace threw a greater strain on Derek and myself who were hauling in the rear, and on the broken surface the sledge overturned several times. We cursed Donald for his cupidity but he went on, heedless of our abusive shouts. Getting no response from Donald we became annoyed with each other. The peak was reached when Derek's right leg slipped into a crevasse up to the knee, and the sledge, skidding fast down an incline, smashed into his leg, trapping him. We were stopped by the jerk and his enraged cry of pain. Long ago we had lost sympathy for each other and I wearily said, "Oh pull your leg out Derek and stop playing for a rest."

"You stupid bastard. How can I, when you bloody idiots won't help? As for you Kinloch, why don't you drop down the nearest crevasse." He was almost beside himself in his pain and anger. In the end we went back to free him, but at least the accident had the effect of slowing Donald up.

As we turned towards the fork we ran into the ridges and *séracs* forced up by the pressure of the ice where the two streams converged; the glacier here resembled the rubble of bomb damage. We had a dreadful time with the sledge, pulling it up and lowering it down ramps and walls, some of them six feet high. We became engaged in an exhausting tug of war with the sledge, which jammed or capsized every few yards. Slowly we struggled on. Fortunately, when the sun became too hot and our patience was exhausted we came upon a level spot amongst the tangle, where it was possible to set up camp. We had brought two tents this time, but even with the luxury of more space and the aid of sleeping pills, we found it impossible to sleep. This was the beginning of the last, and worst, phase of the deadly struggle

against utter fatigue, induced by lack of sleep, which had
been going on for weeks.

The following morning was a glorious contrast to the day
before. The mountains were glittering sugar castles en-
swathed in gossamer veils of cloud, and over the glacier was
spread a low, drifting mist, tinged pink by the early sun in
the north. It was cold and the surface was good. We set off
early, and with only forty pounds or so on our backs, including three days' food, we moved fast and were soon clear of
the *séracs*.

The glacier rose gently and at about halfway went easily
downhill to the foot of McKinley's granite ramparts. It was
seamed with great crevasses which ran right across from one
side to the other. The bridges were enormous and spectacular, but firm, and were no barrier to our progress. We kept
to the center, well away from the area threatened by avalanches which we had often seen break away from the flanks
of Pegasus Peak. From the map, it looked as though there
might be a col at the head of a glacier arm which forced its
way between Koven and Carpé. As we crested the rise of
the main glacier this tributary came into sight, and half an
hour later we were able to see its entire length. It rose very
sharply and the last few hundred feet, up to the col between Koven and Carpé, appeared to be extremely steep.
There was no doubt that the climb would be a difficult one,
but from a camp on the col the ascent of both peaks would
be no problem to a competent party.

We continued up the main glacier until we were close
under the cliffs of McKinley. The towering granite walls
were washed with a rosy hue by the sun's rays. From this
point we could look directly up the ice fall, which tumbled
in a frozen cascade from a plateau high up on the mountain.

The ridge connecting Pegasus Peak and McKinley was now revealed in its entirety. It looked difficult and exacting, its spine a savage tracery of ice, sharply defined against the sky. I felt sure that this would be the crux of the ascent—probably possible only in good conditions. Once beyond it, a party could easily be cut off by bad weather. It was a dangerous route, but a route it was. My hopes of a new way up McKinley, from the Traleika, had been realized. With air drops on McGonagall Pass and the high plateau of Pegasus Peak, McKinley might be climbed in only three weeks from Wonder Lake.

We sat on our packframes in this noble amphitheater, with the mountains rising almost ten thousand feet above us, and scanned the scene with binoculars. A long ridge cleaved its way, in one sweep of ice and snow, to the summit cornice of Pegasus Peak, drawing our attention away from McKinley.

"What a ridge," said Derek, peering through the glasses. "No bother about route-finding, just straight on up to the top. If we could camp here we could attempt Pegasus in say, two days, then cross over and try the col between Koven and Carpé."

He was so enthusiastic about the idea that it caught the imagination of us all. Here were the last prizes within our grasp and we had just enough food to do it. In turn we made an examination of the ridge with the binoculars. It was not as straightforward as it had at first appeared. There were many long ice pitches and the final section was a sheer ice wall. Above this the cornices were enormous and to turn them would take a long time. Nowhere on the ridge did it seem possible to place a camp. Donald thought the route to Koven and Carpé had possibilities, but remained unconvinced of the feasibility of attempting Pegasus Peak from this side.

"I've been studying the route from the Traleika for days," he said. "If we can get across the *séracs* and bergschrund, and the rock will go, we can do it in a day—if conditions are good, I mean."

The rest of us were a little sceptical about this, but we wanted, above all else, to be certain of climbing Pegasus Peak. The only answer was to play safe and concentrate on this one ascent by Donald's route.

Once the decision had been made, we stayed only long enough to collect some rock from McKinley's cliffs before beginning the return. On the whole the journey up the glacier fork had not been unfruitful, and another phase of the exploration program had been completed. Only Derek felt some regrets about returning to the main glacier and voiced his disappointment over our brusque rejection of his route.

We started back to meet the advancing sun which was driving back the shadows and destroying the firm surface of the snow. The crevasse bridges were now decidedly unsafe. Warwick led most of the way back, going down into concealed crevasses three times, once up to his waist. In this last fall he wrenched his ankle badly, which made him limp painfully.

We all had a rather protective feeling for Warwick by now as far as traveling over glaciers was concerned. This was due, no doubt, to the fact that he was the heaviest man and more likely to break through. In the main, however, this feeling sprang from a deep sympathy for him as a result of his two unfortunate accidents: the fall in Wales, and the Albuhera glacier crevasse. In both of these he had just escaped with his life, and it was fairly certain that they had made serious inroads on his store of nervous energy. Yet he took his turns in leading, and his risks, without shirking. When I traveled behind him I fervently hoped all the time that he would not fall. To watch him go down three times that morning was not pleasant. Each time his nerves must have almost screamed with the shock.

By now we had reduced danger to a minimum, and at the first sign of a man in trouble three anchoring axes would drive into the snow simultaneously. Even when we were tired, reactions were very fast, and our glacier travel techniques were almost polished perfection.

It was late when we finally reached the Fork Camp—too late to move on any farther. Lying among the *séracs* and scourged by the sun we spent another day racked with tiredness, but unable to sleep in the airless heat and blinding light.

18.   Pegasus Peak

A FAST JOURNEY back to Raven's Camp was made in the early hours of the next day, the light sledge coming along easily over a good gliding surface of hard snow.

The raven had been a visitor to the camp in our absence. His tracks were everywhere; but he had not been able to penetrate the ice cache, where our last few days' rations were stored. His annoyance at our inhospitality was apparent from the litter of torn-up pieces of paper and cardboard. This rubbish, and the other signs of our habitation, stained the clean glacier surface like a leprous blot.

At five o'clock in the morning, over a hurried lunch snack, we argued about the methods to be employed on Pegasus Peak.

"Don't you see," said Donald, "if we can get up the first bits with no loads and in good conditions, we can make it up and down in a day." He cited various examples of six-thousand-foot Alpine ascents which could be accomplished in a day.

"But this isn't the Alps, Donald," Warwick pointed out. "This is an unknown mountain. The weather is uncertain; we've been in the mountains for nearly six weeks and we're not exactly fresh. Anyway, with my duff ankle you may have to make it with three only."

"Another thing, Donald," put in Derek, "there's the *séracs*, the bergschrund, and the rock. We don't even know if we can get over that lot yet."

"Ah, yes, but I've seen a route which will miss out most of that," Donald said. "It would take us a long way up the glacier before tackling the climb."

"That's miles away," I said. "By the time we've done that, half the day will be over and we'll have to spend the night somewhere on the mountain."

"Why not give it a try? I still say it can be done in a day."

"Yes, perhaps, but not by your route."

Both sides were relenting slightly. We renewed our study of the mountain.

From where we camped, the glacier rose in a ramp which ran along the foot of the peak. Along the whole of its length it was dissected by crevasses. Fringing the glacier was a long strip of *séracs* like dragon's teeth, black decay tingeing their whiteness, and somewhere among them ran the moat of the bergschrund. Above these defenses rose an ice cliff surmounted by a five-hundred-foot wall of friable rock. Lapping over the top of this, like cake icing, a steep snow slope swung upwards to a broad shelf.

From this, even steeper slopes, jutting with ice cliffs, swept up to a large plateau. A long ridge, bordering the far side of the plateau, climbed up to the corniced, flat-topped summit. We were camped at about six thousand five hundred feet and the estimated height of Pegasus Peak was thirteen thousand feet, maybe more. It was a long way to climb on an unknown mountain in one day.

"There is a shorter way up onto the first snow slope, I'm certain," said Derek, putting down the binoculars.

"O.K. then, what about a recce [reconnaissance]?" Donald agreed grudgingly.

"I think we had better assume that it's a two-day job," said Warwick. "If we make up light packs of two days' rations and a tent, plus a sleeping bag, they'll only weigh about thirty pounds. That much weight won't make any difference and it'll make sure that we don't get caught out."

"Warwick's right," I said. "Let's make up the loads and carry them up on the recce to make a dump. That way we'll get a fast start tomorrow."

It was eight o'clock before we had made up four packs, more or less tidy, out of an assortment of rations, stove, fuel, sleeping bags, ropes, tents, route flags, and pitons. By eight-thirty, three of us were on the move, leaving Warwick to rest his ankle. Derek, eager to prove his theory after being outvoted on his other route the day before, pressed on in front.

We marked the route carefully—particularly through the entrapping mesh of crevasses below the *séracs*. Derek went down once, but I checked him and he led on into the piled jumble of ice. Almost exactly where he had expected he found a thin fretwork of ice bridging the bergschrund. Neither the ice wall beyond nor the rock looked unclimbable, and after making a dump of our three packs we started back.

I was in the middle of the rope, and before we had left the crevassed area I muffed my takeoff on a jump across a large fissure, and plummeted down. Luckily, after I had dropped about five feet one of my snowshoes struck a projecting spike of ice. The shock drove me to my knees and I disappeared below the surface. Beneath my feet the crevass opened up into a misty blue abyss, but the rope, tightening on my chest, kept me upright. While I crouched there my imagination plumbed the depths below. I vividly pictured my frozen body lying deep in the glacier, and three figures, silent and sad, moving away towards McGonagall Pass. A delayed chill of fright ran through me, but relieved at my escape, I bobbed to the surface with a smile. At the end of a taut twenty feet of rope, held round an embedded ice axe, Donald looked worried and grim.

"Hullo doctor," I said brightly, "sorry I've kept you waiting. I just dropped down to have a look. There's a very rare hole underneath here."

"It's not at all a laughing matter," reprimanded Donald. "Don't you realize how dangerous it could be?"

"Of course I do, my dear Donald, so would you if you were standing where I am. But as I am still standing, and able to look at your handsome Gaelic face, I feel quite cheerful."

"Ugh! Your false cheerfulness makes me mad," he exploded. "Why aren't you more serious about these things? I could bear it if you were."

"Look, before this ice spike melts, and I go to my death with a brave smile, would you help me out?"

"Blast you; I suppose so."

"There's a good doctor."

When I stood in safety, Donald began to lecture both of us on the dangers of climbing at this time of day. It was nearly midday and the sun's destructive rays were already eating into the *séracs,* which threatened us like tottering ruins. But Donald preached on about the maxims of the Alps and the perils of snow and ice. Derek and I stood uncomfortably under this harangue, keeping an anxious eye on the *séracs.*

Derek said heatedly, "Well, we had to come up and have a look and see if my theory was right, or else we might have been caught out tomorrow. Talk sense, Donald."

"I know we had to come, but we should have come earlier." Donald was even more annoyed.

They snapped on at each other over my head, as I stood in the middle, until I could no longer see the funny side of the argument.

"Donald, there was no other time if we were to pack, and a recce was essential. Derek's route is shorter and possibly puts the climb within a very long day. This is not the Alps and so far we are safe. Let's cut the argument and get back to camp for a meal and some bed."

On the way back, Donald said he thought our nerves had suffered considerably, especially Warwick's. He thought that our store of nervous energy was running low. Derek agreed with him, but I could not fully endorse Donald's opinion. I certainly did not think that Warwick was at such a low ebb. It was true that we had been under considerable strain physically and mentally, but that was inherent in any expedition. Possibly the stress was accentuated in such a small party, when no move anywhere could be made with absolute safety. Most of the time it had been necessary to maintain safety by pooling all our skill, endurance, and courage by moving four on a rope.

There were risks all the way that had to be calculated and taken with the full knowledge of the danger. These and the shocks that all of us had undergone—especially Warwick—had drawn on our vital powers. We had all been close to death at least once in the past weeks. We were all imaginative men and we suffered more for it, but a man without imagination would not last.

Each one of us has only so much nervous energy and it is a vital factor and should be husbanded carefully. In times of stress the mind must be toughened and steeled against surprise. The impact of shock and strain should be taken up by the immediate level of consciousness, retaining the core of the episode cushioned on the resilient upper strata of the mind. For if it pierces the more sensitive layers of thought and memory, its reverberations will sully the store of nervous energy and weaken the resolve.

Warwick had supper ready when we got back to camp,

and we ate it sitting outside on the upturned sledge. In the
north and south ominous clouds, in angry shapes, were
building up and beginning to advance on each other.
The sun oppressed us, and in the turmoil of heated air small,
low-lying clouds began to rise vertically up the mountainside. By the time we went to our tents, to try and sleep with
the aid of drugs, a wind had sprung up. It was the same story
as on previous days. We lay in the tents only lightly clothed
and hoped for drugged oblivion. The wind, increasing in
strength, made it impossible to open the tent entrances.
The trapped heat of the day was stifling. With ever increasing frequency gusts dashed themselves into the tent until it
danced and shook, the cloth rattling like parchment. Under
this beating some of the pegs came away and the guy ropes
lashed the tent like whips in frenzied hands. I crawled out
into the wind. The moving air was full of snow, blasted up
from the glacier surface. The anemometer was registering
more than sixty knots, and it took a long time to secure
the guys. When I dropped down beside Warwick again,
I felt worn out.

The racketing of the tent, and the heat, made sleep quite
impossible.

"You asleep, Warwick?" I asked.

"No, it's going to be another deadly night."

I turned over and looked at the black-bearded face and
the bleary, bloodshot eyes.

"I'm dying for a drink, what about a brew of lemon?"

"O.K. I'll have to get the stove from the others."

Donald was awake, but Derek was furious at being wakened, although he soon fell asleep again. Because of the
wind we had to use the stove inside the tent. The temperature
at the roof rose from a just bearable 110°F to 150°F. When
I crouched near the stove my skin felt dry and like tinder. It

was like standing at the open door of a furnace. As soon as the snow had melted I put the stove out, mixed the lemon, then lay back gasping. The cold drink tasted heavenly and I passed half of it to the others.

The alarm clock was by my face and I watched the minutes and hours drag past until seven-thirty, when I must have fallen asleep. An hour later the alarm drilled into my ear and I sat up, eyes smarting with tiredness. The temperature outside was 37°F and we could hear the avalanches roaring down almost continuously. We had a hurried consultation, shouting between the tents, and decided to wait until ten o'clock. There was no sleep after this, and every two hours we checked the thermometer, but the temperature remained above freezing. The wind dropped and a light mist came down, damping the sound of the avalanche barrage which rolled on, sometimes frighteningly near. We decided that this was not the day.

At four o'clock Derek said, "Supposing the raven attacks the dump. All our food's up there."

"He'd be a bloody fool to be up there in this weather," said Warwick churlishly.

Nevertheless it was a worrying thought, and half an hour later the three of us were off up to the dump, leaving Warwick still resting his ankle. After making sure that the bergschrund bridge still existed we returned with the packs. It felt like a retreat.

For the rest of the morning we packed the sledge for the march out. A minimum of four hundred pounds remained after discarding all nonessentials.

Warwick's ankle had responded well to rest and he thought it would stand up to the climb. This cheered him somewhat and in an expansive mood, as cook, he mixed into a drink two well-known nighttime beverages. He handed the mixture round apprehensively. "It's quite beautifully disgusting, but full of O.K. stuff." It tasted like very old dishwater.

When we went to bed, clouds were tumbling over Charybdis Col to be sucked down into a maelstrom of wind and storm which raged, half hidden by the flank of Pegasus Peak, at the head of the glacier. The wind rose sharply and was soon shrieking around us, hurling the drift into the tents. The temperature was lower, but I could not sleep. I rolled over and over, sometimes turning to stare into Warwick's open, fixed eyes. Thoughts chased each other round my brain, whirling and jostling uncontrollably.

. . . *If we don't get up Pegasus tonight, then that's it. There won't be time for a second attempt. We must allow two days. If it takes two days we'll only have a day and a half to pack up and get out.* . . . The tent rattled and shook. The sides closed in, then ballooned outwards. The clock ticked remorselessly in my ear. Twelve-thirty . . . *If we don't get out on time a whole rescue attempt will be set up. Think of the repercussions in Ottawa and the War Office! Without Pegasus climbed, the main aim of the expedition will be left unfinished. This one peak will set the seal on the work.*

"Asleep, Jimmy?"

"No, can't shut my eyes. This blasted wind. Got a drink?"

"Yes, in my bottle, here you are."

"Thanks."

The water tasted harsh but it soothed my dry throat. *Have we done enough? I suppose so, there's no doubt about it, the only way to finance an expedition is to put up the money yourself, then you don't have to worry about producing results in return for other people's cash. I wonder if Warwick's ankle will be all right? If it goes on the climb, or on the withdrawal, we'll never get out on time.*

If we'd brought two small tarpaulins, one for the wind break and one to keep off the sun, we could have slept outside. But they would never have stayed up in this wind. We've never even had time in these last few weeks to build an igloo. That would be the answer to this sleep business but it's the time . . . time . . . time. . . . Two-thirty. . . . The time to explore in these mountains is between late March and mid-June—no later. Then at least for the first two months the temperatures are low enough to move in the day. Then the routine would be normal and sleep no problem. We arrived a month too late, really. Still it couldn't be helped; we couldn't have got ready sooner, and with the long journey. . . .

I turned over again; Warwick's back was towards me.

"Asleep, Warwick?"

"No, not a hope."

"I wonder if the others are awake?"

"I wonder. Donald! Derek! Are you awake?"

There was no answer.

"Lucky monsters."

. . . If only we could have got our lift from the Canadians, we'd have been here by mid-May. Ah well. . . . I wish I'd taken a supply drop from the U.S.A.F. It would have been worth at least four or five extra days. We could have got more done. I wonder if we have done enough? If we don't get up Pegasus tonight. . . .

So I lay fretting, my mind in a turmoil. Sleep, the only release, would not come.

I lay staring up at the billowing, jerking, green cloth and the thermometer tied to the roof, flailing about on the end of its string. I tried reading, but the recurring thoughts chased the meaning of the words from my brain. The feverish fantasy of question and answer danced on in my mind and I seemed utterly remote from my body. In ob-

jective detachment I looked down upon myself, lying prostrate in the greenish light, enclosed by the contracting and
swelling skin of the tent. After sleepless days of continual
physical and mental strain, there was no vitality left, no
determination, only sheer apathy and acceptance; to be
able to sleep was all. So this was why brain-washed prisoners
convicted themselves out of their own mouths.

At eight-thirty the alarm forced me into action—it was
a relief to do something. Warwick was awake immediately
—out of a brief doze—and we woke the others. They had
apparently slept for several hours. As we spooned the brose
from our cups we debated whether or not to attempt the
mountain. It was cold, but the wind, although gusting
strongly, had lessened in force. Warwick and I argued that
it was almost certain to be blowing a gale higher up and
that any attempt on the mountain would be foolhardy and
bound to fail. The other two insisted that at least we might
take a look and get as high as possible. The truth was—although Warwick and I did not care to admit it—that we
were more concerned about ourselves than about climbing
the mountain. Desperately tired, unsure about our strength
and fearing a breakdown, we buttressed our weak arguments with empty, pompous talk of "good mountaineering
judgment." Without us the other two could not go. When
pressed to make a decision I hedged and dithered pitifully.
Finally, shamed by the enthusiasm and determination of
the sleep-refreshed Derek and Donald, I agreed that we
should go.

Just before eleven o'clock we started out up the glacier.
Four figures, roped together, hooded, and crouching against
the wind, we moved through the flying drift. The wind was
in our faces, like a knife on the exposed flesh, flattening the
clothes to our bodies, rattling the tiny particles of ice and
snow against the stiff windproofs. Unseen, hidden from us

by the mass of the mountain, a storm was raging. If it was sweeping the slopes of Pegasus Peak above the rock, the attempt would come to a standstill. I half hoped that this would happen.

The route flags led us safely through the puzzle of crevasses. The delicate arch of ice, now known as Pritchard's Peril, still bridged the bergschrund. Once across, a route up the ice cliffs now disclosed itself to us and we took it, grateful for the escape from the slow labor of step-cutting. Below the looming rock wall we split into two ropes. Donald and Warwick started off first, climbing carefully up the rotten face, moving one at a time. A stone dislodged by the two above fell without warning and struck Derek's arm with a painful thud. Others followed, just missing his head, so we moved out of the line of fire. We started upwards, keeping well clear of the leading pair. The angle was not great, but our progress was slow; no hold could be trusted.

We reached the top soon after Donald and Warwick but, while we were putting on our crampons, they moved off and climbed steadily up the first slope and were lost to sight over the crest. The snow was hard and held the spikes firmly. I led Derek upwards, moving with a slow, easy rhythm. My tiredness had gone. Now, after three hours' climbing, I felt fresh and eager to climb the peak. When we emerged on the shelf the wind hit us again with its bitterly cold blast. We plugged on, bowed against its force. At times the gusts, like great enclosing hands, brought our progress to a halt, or swung us staggering from our tracks, but we kept on upwards.

The others were well in front, climbing with a remorseless purpose up and around the ice cliffs. We stopped occasionally to film them. Soon we, too, were among the cliffs and had lost sight of them again. At intervals we put in route flags and took bearings—which I wrote down in my notebook—from one to the other. Without them, if mist overtook us on the descent, route-finding on such a broad sweep of cliff, cluttered with ice and snow, would be almost impossible and very dangerous.

The slope grew steeper as we drew near the top, and on occasional ice pitches we were forced to nick small steps. At the top we wound our way through the castellated ice to gain the upper plateau. Here the others waited, and as we plodded towards them, through deep powder snow, mist rolled over us and with it the wind returned. Rushing with its wild force over the desolate plateau it struck with its deadly cold. We had been climbing for over six hours and Donald suggested that we make a halt to eat in some sheltered place. A few yards farther on we found a snow-filled crevasse which gave us some protection from the gale.

The cold began to creep into us and we pressed ourselves into the snow to try and gain warmth, or stamped our feet and flailed our arms. Donald, as cook for the day, produced some butter and cheese. He took a long time to open a tin of cheese, for he could not risk his bared hands for more than a few seconds. We ate the frozen butter like a sweet; the yellow lumps splintered in our mouths, brittle and tasteless.

In less than half an hour the cold had driven us to move off again. The wind had quitted the plateau almost as suddenly as it had arrived, and gaps in the mist appeared fleetingly. For a moment we saw the ridge in profile as it marched to the unseen summit. A steep buttress fell from it up which we might climb direct to the top, avoiding the dangers of the wind-embattled ridge. Before the mist cleared again we took a quick compass bearing on the buttress and began the march towards it. Derek and I took over the lead and floundered on through the deep powder snow. Suddenly I felt tired. Fatigue swept over me and every step be-

came an immense labor. Never before had I felt the strength
go out of me quite so suddenly. There had always been
some warning and the gradual onset of tiredness. But not
now; I was suddenly at the limit. There was only determination left with which to bend each weakened knee, raise the
weighted feet, and force the body forward. The mist began
to clear, but I dared not look up in case the climb ahead
appalled me and weakened my will.

At the bergschrund, which lay a little way up the buttress, we halted and watched the others as they followed
our tracks. Warwick's head was down and his movements
had the hesitant, unsteady look of tiredness. He flopped
down beside me, his face haggard, his eyes dull and fixed.

"You look about as shagged as I feel," I said.

He nodded and hunched forward, his arms resting on his
knees. The other two felt almost fresh, owing, no doubt, to
the sleep which had been denied Warwick and me. It was
fortunate that they felt fit enough to chaperone us to the
summit.

Beyond the bergschrund the buttress rose with unrelenting steepness into the mist. The snow was hard and Derek
began to kick small toeholds upwards. It was no doubt the
easiest and quickest way to climb, but I did not feel equal
to this delicate, fast tiptoeing and was forced to put in two
or three more kicks to improve each one of his indentations.
Every extra effort taxed me terribly, and I appealed to
him to kick proper steps. To my complete surprise, and utter gratitude, he happily accepted this extra labor, and
above me large pigeonholes began to appear in the packed
snow. For a while I was content to clamber after him. Soon,
however, I was reduced to going up ten steps at a time and
then resting. Gradually, by forcing my feeble legs to further
efforts, I increased the number of steps, making my breathing spaces even longer. I would climb a dozen or fifteen

until I was only a few feet below Derek. Then I would rest, bent over my axe, watching the loop of rope, which hung below me, gradually drawn into a straight upward line. Just before it grew taut I would make a short spurt upwards again and then rest. In this way I was able to keep going.

Hour after hour we climbed, the angle of about forty-five degrees never changing. I stepped up, rested, and stepped up again, the looping rope my timekeeper and taskmaster. My thoughts were far away in England, dreaming of the brief holiday I would have on return, driving with Jeanne in my new car, floating with superb ease along the country lanes. It was the greatest contrast which my tired mind could devise to the labor on this never ending white ramp. Even Derek's legs were tiring, and every hundred feet or so we would halt, cut little platforms to sit on, and watch the others slowly toil up to us.

At some halts Warwick fell asleep as soon as he sat down and had to be wakened by Donald before they could go on. Near to what we thought was the top, Donald and Warwick took over, and as the buttress widened and the snow softened they went upwards in long zigzag traverses. Donald strained upwards, determination in every line of his body. He seemed to surge forward, translating his power into an inexorable rhythm, thrusting himself towards the summit, trailing after him the mute, hooded, automaton that was Warwick.

A cry from Donald and a wave of his axe announced that the summit was in sight. Soon we all stood together at the point where the buttress joined the ridge. A few hundred yards away to our left the ridge ended in the great cornice, which gave the peak its flat-topped summit. Derek filmed the others as they completed the climb, and then we joined them.

When I arrived on the summit I began to gain some

strength, but my feelings were more of relief than elation. The wind shrilled around us in a freezing-cold blast. The temperature was well below zero and ice had formed under my anorak. For odd moments the wind tore aside the veil of mist and we caught, in fragmentary pictures, glimpses of mountains about us. The Traleika Glacier, revealed for one long view, appeared black-ribbed, riven with the upthrust of conflicting pressures, and seamed with the dark lines of open crevasses. We could only guess at the trials of the march out. I buried a red airborne beret with a note and took the ritual photograph of our flag. Warwick, ever the kind uncle of the expedition, produced a tin of jam which he mixed with snow. It was a refreshing confection.

The cold drove us from the summit and we began the descent. Each pair was on a long rope and we began a series of sitting glissades. We moved singly, one man protecting the other with an axe belay. These rapid swoops took us quickly down the buttress.

At about the halfway mark, when he was still well above me, Derek suddenly lost control and shot forward head-first, rolling over and over down the slope. The nylon whirred round my axe. I pressed my weight down heavily on the head and began to retard the runout of the rope. With about thirty feet of rope to go I checked him. My axe was levered back towards me and the rope stretched like elastic. He stopped in a peculiar twisted position for a moment I thought he had broken a limb in the fall. I called down to him. Presently he sat up, drove his axe in, and secured himself. When I reached him I saw that blood was trickling from a small square puncture in his forehead where his axe point had struck, just missing his eye.

Chastened by this experience, we continued the descent on foot. But the mountain was in a vindictive mood, and shortly afterwards I was astonished to find myself waist-

deep in a crevasse. The chapter of accidents was not finished. A few hundred feet lower, as I was following Derek
down, a crampon spike caught in my trouser leg. I tripped
and fell, falling forward headfirst. I felt my arms and legs
flailing uncontrollably as I rolled and bounced downwards.
I kept the axe in my hand. Somehow I managed to straighten
my body and get my head upwards. Rolling over onto my
stomach I began to brake my progress by digging in the
point of the axe. Just when I was beginning to congratulate
myself on this recovery, I shot over the top of an ice cliff.

As I was launched outwards I looked up despairingly to
see Derek with his axe in, belaying me. But such was the
speed of my fall that I concluded quite dispassionately
that there was not much chance of his holding me. For a
moment as I turned in the air I saw down the entire length
of the buttress. The bergschrund was a thin, wavering hair-
line in the snow. There was a split-second, sickening seizure
of panic; then I hit the hard snow in a tangle of rope, limbs,
pack, and ice axe. The one thought in my mind was that I
must roll on my stomach and get the axe in. After a few more
feet the axe pick was skidding through the snow and then
there was a tremendous dragging pull on my chest and I
stopped. Derek had held me. I stood up feeling slightly
bruised and considerably shaken. I had fallen about two
hundred feet. My first feelings were of exhilaration at the
success of our efforts in averting disaster after the first care-
less mistake. A moment later they were submerged in a wave
of horrified relief which swept over me. Derek came down
to where I stood and I thanked him in the half-embarrassed
way which always seems so completely inadequate on these
occasions.

We continued our descent even more cautiously, meeting up with the others by our lunch place. Donald, with a
shield-shaped patch over his nose to protect it and his face

almost hidden with scarf, balaclava, and goggles, looked exactly like the Scottish cartoon-strip character.

"Well, Rank," I said, "do you think we can risk the ice cliffs below?"

"Oh, I think so," he replied from under the mask. "With the wind and the cold it'll be safe. You see, we'll make it in a day."

It looked as though we would, too.

Derek asked Warwick how he was feeling.

"Fit enough to get down anyway," he said. "I've been feeling fine since the summit."

"The clot took a benzedrine and didn't tell me," said Donald, professionally severe. "We'll have to watch it on this last bit when we get tired."

Roped four together for added security, we found our way through the ice cliffs, traversing this way and that until we reached the easier gradients of the shelf. In our weary state we were almost excessively cautious on the rock, concentrating all our attention on the placing of hands and feet. In a small niche Warwick found the only plant life we had seen in the glacier—a small pink flower clinging to the rock. He took several specimens and I photographed this small tenacious plant which clung to the rock and somehow survived in a hostile, dead world.

Luckily, the ice bridge still held and we plodded thankfully down the last stretch of glacier and into camp. We had been out nearly nineteen hours.

"There you are," said Donald jubilantly, as we took off our snowshoes and coiled the ropes, "up and back in a day. It takes a lot to disprove Alpine experience."

There seemed to be nothing more to say.

19. *The Withdrawal*

WE ALL slept that night, but I was surprised to awake after only six hours. I had expected to be dead to the world for at least twelve. Only the dormouselike Derek found it difficult to get up.

We could take out only a light sledge load and about fifty pounds each on our backs. The equipment and our spare clothes were carefully sorted and the essentials packed. They included all the results of the scientific program and Donald's spring balance. By noon all was finished and Donald had cajoled us into doing a last step test.

For seven hours, between two and nine o'clock in the evening, Warwick and I again clutched unsuccessfully at elusive sleep. Derek and Donald fared little better. When we arose we all felt listless and weak.

It was midnight when we strained forward in our harnesses and the sledge began to glide over the hard snow. We left the old green Meade tent standing there. Inside were some clothing, Warwick's broken camera, and a note. In the dying rays of the sun, with its walls rattling at the light touch of the breeze, we left it for the last time—an almost pathetic reminder of our transient presence in the utter loneliness of the frozen mountain silence.

Ahead lay a stretch of glacier up which we had toiled,

in relays, for over ten days to reach this place. Now we had thirty-six hours in which to get down beyond Helicopter Camp into Cache Creek. That was the price of Pegasus Peak. We had almost no food and we relied on picking up the three days' ration at Creaking Camp. There was little chance that our dump at Helicopter Camp would be intact; it was low enough to be reached by marauding wolverine, or even bear. There was also a small dump of clothes and odds and ends near Crevasse Camp, but no food.

For the first two hours we made steady progress. The lightly laden sledge came along easily, and crevasses were either obvious or had safe bridges. Near the fork the glacier began to change into a tumbled rubble of *séracs* and ice waves. Man-hauling became impossible. We were forced to manhandle the sledge over the obstacles, and for long stretches it had to be carried. By six o'clock we had to admit reluctantly that the sledge had outlived its purpose; it was now a hindrance to our progress. We could take it no further. The sledge load was shared out and strapped to our packs after careful weighing to ensure that no one was unfairly handicapped. When we started off once more we were each carrying over ninety pounds.

Gradually the snow gave way to bare glacier ice and we changed our snowshoes for crampons. The direction of our course was confirmed when we came unexpectedly upon Warwick's "Fred's Snack Bar" sign. For the first time we were at a recognizable point of our journey up the glacier, and as we looked around us we began to realize the enormous changes brought about by the thaw. The glacier was changed almost out of all recognition. Before us, stretching across the glacier, lay the gaping crevasses. The ribs running down the glacier—which we had seen from Pegasus Peak—were, in fact, three lines of enormous, moraine-covered *séracs*, one at each side and one in the middle.

We slogged on under the hot sun, our crampons biting securely into the honeycombed ice. By the time we had reached the dump by Crevasse Camp we had become expert at jumping the small crevasses which occurred every few yards, but were not, any of them, more than six feet wide. We were roped together and one man jumped at a time. At first, as each man jumped, the others stood by protecting him, but this was too slow and after a while the whole rope kept on the move, each man taking the crevasses in his stride.

At the dump we loaded a few more pounds onto our packs and stripped down to shirtsleeves. We rested for a while, looking up the glacier at the high clouds moving slowly around the summit of Pegasus Peak and drifting lazily over Charybdis Col. Then on again, the loads bowing us down, the straps biting viciously into our shoulders. The great rifts in the ice grew so large that we could not jump them, and we wandered up and down their sides searching for a way across. When there was a sagging bridge of old grey snow we would venture across, our feet pressing through the soggy surface; we tried to achieve a breathless form of levitation, the tight rope between us communicating the tension. Sometimes, at the first thrust of the testing axe, or the pressure of a foot, the bridge would give up its tenuous hold on the icy sides, and with a soft slithering noise the snow would buckle and fall into the depths. To cross some of the crevasses we cut steps down inside, then stepped across and climbed out. In the center of others there was often a pillar of ice onto which we would jump, landing one-footed to spring without pause to the other side.

In spite of our packs we achieved a catlike sense of balance and timing. Crevasses which earlier we would have thought twice about before jumping without loads, we now hurled ourselves across with our dragging burdens. Once, when confronted with the possibility of being cut off, we moved only a hundred yards in an hour and a half, but by sheer dogged determination we found a way through.

Hour after hour we continued, sometimes balancing on knife-edges to circumvent the chasms, at others jumping double crevasses separated only by a thin strip of ice, or trusting our judgment to land on impossibly narrow ledges. All this was over blue-black gaping voids, alternating a ballerinalike precision with a fast, laden, shambling gait over the unbroken sections. Never was any move made unprotected. Our understanding was complete, the rope a double bond of trust and security between us.

After thirteen hours we came to the site of Creaking Camp. There were few signs of our former occupation. The place was a chaos of cracked ice and there was no trace of the food dump. It must have been swallowed up long ago. The clouds were lower and the wind chill. We pulled on extra clothes over our sweat-soaked bodies as we waited for Derek to cook lunch.

From potato-mash powder, dates, dried bananas, and butter he concocted a memorable meal. We washed it down with nectarlike tea. For a while we rested among the shambles of moraine, rocks, and ice, enjoying the relief from the packs. I studied the sweat-stained faces of the others. They looked older and utterly weary. We had lost, some time ago, the perfectly tuned fitness of the athlete; we were tired and worn and we needed rest. But we had achieved a hardness of mind and body which was equal to any demands, On that day, with our goal before us, we were capable of anything.

We moved off again with sweaters or scarves under the pack straps to relieve our shoulders. Warwick had even cut up his precious bath mat for use as pads. Gradually the crevasses became narrow, or crossing places easier to find, as we resumed our laden steeplechase down the glacier. As we landed after each jump the crushing weight of the packs drove us to our knees. The strain on our legs and ankles was tremendous. The packframes buckled and wrenched our aching backs and shoulders.

After an hour or so the crevasses dwindled to mere cracks in the glacier and our progress was almost unimpeded. Over the bare ice and moraine we continued with scarcely a halt. My back was a mass of dull pain; my packframe had fractured under the strain and the load hung unevenly. To get some relief I had tried the tump line, but it came off when I jumped. The pace increased, and at times we jogged along at a shuffling run. Although there was now no danger, we were still roped together—it seemed almost unnatural for the rope to be off.

At last we came onto the flat moraine which curved round to Helicopter Camp. When we thought that we must be near we stopped and scanned the rocks with binoculars —and there it was, only a few hundred yards away! The food, the films, the odd bits of clothing, they were all there; the cache was intact. In the somber light of the lowering sky the strained faces looked happy. We congratulated each other. In an hour the tent was up and we were eating a glorious bully beef stew.

After the meal I walked a short distance along the moraine and stood looking up at the cloud-filled Traleika. I remembered the day I had arrived there and emerged from the warm cacophony of helicopter noise into the strange silence of the mountains. I pictured the glacier as it was on the first day we had sledged out. The rocks on which I stood then had been smooth-surfaced with snow. I thought of how we had traveled and lived, up there beyond the clouds. Now I could see no further than a mile or so up the flank of Tatum. The clouds hid from me what had once been our own. In the dull grey light I walked back to the tent, filled with a deep sadness.

We allowed ourselves just over three hours' sleep and rose in the early morning to find a dismal wet mist sitting on the moraine. When the quick breakfast was eaten, Donald made a ceremonial burning of his shattered showshoes and we fed the flames with the cardboard boxes and meta fuel tablets from the cache. For a few brief moments flames shot their dancing points of light into the mist. It was a symbolic farewell to the Traleika.

We descended into the trough which lay like a ditch along the line of *séracs*. It was dotted with small glacial lakes on which a few frozen-looking ducks huddled. Skirting these we cramponed down the steep incline and came to the first defenses of the *séracs*, which marked the junction of the Traleika and Muldrow glaciers. This, we thought, was the last barrier before the clear run across the ice to the McGonagall Pass.

Crowding close upon one another, with their steep sides and tottering masses of ice, the *séracs* posed a difficult problem. We cut steps, made short vertical ascents, trotted along sharp knife-edges, and leapt more fearsome chasms like humpbacked, claw-footed demons. As we surmounted the last row of these giant dragon's teeth we saw, beyond another strip of smooth ice, a chain of vast moraine heaps rising up like miniature blackened Alps. We flung ourselves desperately at these, but our force was soon dissipated with seeking a way through the devious jumble. Hours were spent in grinding our way up steep faces, crampons clashing with the rocks. Again, and again, we thought that the end was in sight, only to see another wave of filthy mounds barring the way. Underneath, torrents of water ran gushing like a glacial sewer. Eaten up with frustration we cursed all glaciers, *séracs*, and moraines, in a ceaseless flow of bad-tempered language. Then, quite unexpectedly, the last vile black slopes ran down to the whiteness of the Muldrow. Away on the other side we could see the mist-enshrouded pass. Under the lowering clouds, which rested only a few hundred feet up the mountainsides, we crossed the bare ice quickly.

The edge of the glacier was in sight when we heard, somewhere above the mist, an aircraft engine. Derek flung off his pack and took out the radio.

"Tell him we're almost across the Muldrow and that we'll be down at four thousand feet in Cache Creek at noon," I said. Derek repeated the message. The aircraft droned away and then returned; it seemed to be circling overhead.

"Hello, British mountaineering party calling. British mountaineering party calling. The cloud base is down to five hundred feet. We can't see you. We are near McGonagall Pass. If you can receive and understand us rev your engines."

We heard the engine note rise up to a roar and then die again.

"Mountaineering party to aircraft, we heard that. Thank you."

"It was the SA-16, I'm damn sure," said Derek. "At least they know we're on the way."

"Yes, but if these clouds get any lower, or the weather gets worse, they may not be able to get in to us," Warwick said, sounding a note of caution.

"All I want to do is to walk along unroped, side by side, just chatting, with no snow or crevasses to worry about," I said, "and the sooner the better. So let's get on."

I led off on the last few yards. McGonagall Pass seemed very near. Then I topped a rise and saw the water. A long lake, with an island in the middle, lay between the glacier and the far shore.

"Oh no. This is the end. We'll have to swim to get out of these blasted mountains," I groaned.

"No one told us about this," moaned Derek.

"There's probably an easy way onto the glacier from the Pass, but not many people have come this way before," said Donald.

The worry and frustration of it was almost laughable.

We trekked down the glacier to where the lake narrowed, seeking a way off the ice, but ice cliffs fell straight to the water. Turning back, we marched alongside the dismal mere through the soft snow which fringed the ice shore. A broken plastic sledge lying there gave us the idea of rowing across, but the shallow vessel was too unstable.

Donald was in the lead now, and much to his disgust we began to cross crevasses. The belaying and the cautious movement started all over again. It began to rain—lashing rods of cold water which soaked us to the skin. The others were quiet, but when they spoke, the sharp urgency of their voices betrayed their nervousness. I was almost beside myself with the agonizing frustration of it all. I felt angry at the mountains for this last vindictive trick. My pent-up feelings cried out for release; I felt like thrashing the snow with my ice axe and shouting abuse at this unkind mountain world. I did neither, but remained silent and bitter. I began to feel very, very tired.

Slowly we edged along the cliff top, seeking an escape route. At last Donald announced success with a cry of, "We can abseil off this ——— here." I looked over. Below the cliff the gap between the ice and earth narrowed and the stream was bridged by a huge ice floe.

In a frenzy Donald hammered in a piton. With desperate hands he uncoiled the spare rope and, snatching the other, from which we had unclipped ourselves, tied the two together and passed them through the karabiner on the piton. He had his crampons on first and with a gurgling cry of delight abseiled off. From the top we saw him land on the ground, dash across the ice bridge, and kiss a large boulder on the other side. He turned and shouted up to us, "I hope I never see a crevasse again." His face bore an expression of rapturous delight.

"Donald's really steamed up," said Warwick. "He'll go so far and then just die on us."

"Well, as long as he doesn't blow up before we get to Cache Creek I don't mind," I answered wearily.

I was the last man down. The rope stuck in a crack and I could not release it, but Warwick and Donald with a mighty heave pulled it down plus piton.

"Lucky it didn't come out when you were coming down," roared the crazed Donald heartily. I regarded him sourly as I coiled the rope. He could hardly wait to be on the move again. He hopped about, filled with a nervous, agitated energy.

"Look, Donald, it's twelve o'clock now. If you bashed off you could get to Cache Creek and watch for the helicopter." I thought it best to let him get away.

"Right, see you down there." He was off, shouting the words over his shoulder. Derek followed close behind; following Warwick, I toiled across the rocks to the Pass.

Along the lakeside lay signs of the passage of past expeditions to McKinley. Rusty tins, shattered tent poles, boxes, and old fuel cans lay moldering among the rocks. This sad debris of man's violation of nature, in his struggle against it, made the shore of the dismal mere an even more forlorn and desolate place. I was glad to be away from it and to reach the top of the Pass.

From here Warwick and I took a last look across the glacier. The clouds were lower and the mist licked at the ice.

It was a grim, forbidding scene. Far away an avalanche roared, the sound rolling down the glacier. The clouds gave the veiled mountains a sinister appearance. The air seemed full of hidden menace.

"They're bloody hard mountains," said Warwick.

We fled down the rock and snow to find an animal trail which ran beside the creek. At frequent intervals we stopped for rest. We were tired and the packs dragged painfully at our shoulders. When I took my eyes off the ground I stumbled and fell over. The valley gradually opened out and presently we came upon the others who were waiting for us. Donald was wearing his mosquito-net face veil, and both he and Derek were liberally coated with ointment to keep off the ferocious insects. They swirled around our heads in whining halos. Warwick and I soon applied ointment and joined the others in pawing the air, attempting frantically to deter the mosquitos from attacking.

We moved on again straight across country, the track having petered out. To be free of the rope after weeks of being tied one to the other gave me a wonderful sense of freedom. It was sheer joy to feel the earth underfoot and to smell living plants again. With long, easy strides Warwick and I strolled across the heather, side by side, talking.

On a bank just above the stream, where we had a clear view down the valley, we pitched the tent and waited. The rain began again and as we sat eating our last few biscuits, pools of water began to form on the floor. We huddled together in our wet clothes and dozed fitfully. The clouds had cleared a little and we thought that we could see Wonder Lake, but when, at four o'clock, the helicopter had not arrived we resigned ourselves to walking out. I sat by the entrance, my head on my knees, debating whether or not to undress and get into my sleeping bag. Then I thought I heard, in the air, far away, the faint hum of an aircraft en-

gine. Thrusting my head out I saw, a long way off, a four-
engined transport cruising back and forth across the sky.
Below, and much nearer, was the helicopter, like a silver
globe just above the horizon.

"They're here!"

Pandemonium.

We tumbled out of the tent like rabbits from a warren.
I talked on the radio giving our position, while Warwick lit
the three remaining flares, and in accordance with our pre-
arranged plan Donald and Derek packed. The orange and
blue smoke mingled and drifted across the heather as I
crouched in front of the tent jabbering into the set. I had no
idea whether the helicopter was on our net or not. The
machine swung onto a new course and came directly towards us, dropping slowly down, coming to rest after a lop-
sided hop about fifty yards away. The blades continued to
whicker round. I bounded across the ground towards it
still holding my mug of tea, all tiredness gone. Two figures
jumped out; the photographers were in at the end. I reached
the door through the wall of air thrown up by the blades
and picked up the helmet headset.

"Glad to see you. We'd almost given you up."

"Hiya captain. Yeah, the weather held us up. We can
take two out at a time with a little kit. But it'll have to be
fast. This cloud is liable to come down at any moment."

"They're on their way."

Derek and Donald came running towards us, packs on
their backs, clothing and odd things under their arms. They
bundled into the helicopter; as soon as the door was closed
it rose up and veered away down the valley.

We offered the photographers some strong, reddish-
colored tea and invited them inside the tent. They looked
inside at the shambles to which we had grown so accus-
tomed and said, "Thank you, no." It occurred to me that

perhaps we also smelt a little. They crouched outside and said how sorry they were at not being able to get up to see us on the glacier. They had not even been able to get a light plane to come down low to photograph our camp. We started to pack and they took some photographs. They left in the next helicopter lift and we moved all the kit down to the landing place.

We sat pensively sipping tea, our thoughts still up there in the hidden mountains. The helicopter reappeared low in the sky.

"The taxi's here again," said Warwick, standing up. "It all seems to have worked like a charm."

"Yes, it certainly has. I thought more than once it wasn't going to, though. But here we are without a scratch."

"Only just; we've been lucky. At any rate the U.S.A.F. is on the ball."

So they were. By helicopter and seaplane we were whisked across the fairy-tale horror of the tundra to Minchumina by way of Wonder Lake. Here was Henry Coile and his "Goony Bird" Dakota.

"We've been here since dawn waiting for the weather to lift so that we could come in and get you. Why man," he continued, looking at Warwick's beard, "that sure is a dudy-du piece of garbage you've got on there."

In the aircraft we laughed again at his "gypsies' warning," about action to be taken when the "Abandon Aircraft" warning bell sounded.

"When that bell goes you-all get out, and if you see me going past, then boy, you're on your own."

The Dakota landed smoothly at Ladd and rolled to a halt outside the Base Operations Room at nine o'clock that evening. The U.S.A.F. had employed one four-engined transport, one twin-engined amphibian, a Dakota, a seaplane, a helicopter, and thirty men to get us out.

20. The Return

EFFICIENT to the end, the Air Force provided a large station wagon to take us and our kit back to Murphy Hall. Jackson R. Glantz was not there, but the clerk on duty showed no surprise at our appearance and we were rather disappointed when the television-watchers in the hall did not even look up as we slouched in.

We admired our whiskery, tanned, and somewhat wild-eyed faces in the mirror. I have never been very impressed by the sanctity of Queen's Regulations number 1,615, and before leaving England I had read an article about loss of heat through the head, which restrained me from having my hair shorn. With this shaggy three-months' growth, my red beard, sunken cheeks, and overbright eyes I looked like one of the more disreputable Old Testament prophets. A shave removed most of the disguise, and a long soak in the bath, reading my bundle of mail, completed the transformation. There was just time to get a snack in the canteen before it closed. Then complete collapse in the too-soft bed.

Sunday on the base passed quietly and Monday brought the ubiquitous Fred Milan. He had just returned from five months spent living with Lapps in Northern Norway and Sweden. Most of the time he had been moving with them over long distances on skis, and his walk still bore the signs of this method of travel—so much so that as we followed him down the long corridors of Murphy Hall he still appeared to be wearing an imaginary pair of skis.

That evening we gave a party to all those who had helped us at Ladd. It was the only practical way of expressing our gratitude. Our guests showed their appreciation of the gesture in the equally practical manner of Americans when confronted by Scotch whisky. We were finally evicted by an armed orderly officer. The party continued incoherent, confused, and half-remembered in Fred Milan's log cabin, in some near-by wilderness. We were sustained until the small hours by a remarkable supper, deftly produced by Fred—who claimed unique medicinal and restorative properties for it—of tea, Grape-nuts, and cough drops.

At six o'clock the same morning, in a fragile state and in dire need of some Milan restorer, we just scrambled onto the plane for Whitehorse, with seconds to spare.

The Canadian army at Whitehorse, with magnificent generosity, which saved us pounds, provided a car to take us to Dawson Creek. Our heavy kit was to follow by truck. In the luxury of a sumptuous Ford we began the nine-hundred-mile journey down the Alaska Highway. The Highway, a strip of graveled road, runs fifteen hundred miles from Dawson Creek to Fairbanks through wild and, in parts, unexplored country. Built by the Americans during the war, with complete disregard for cost, it was pushed through the wilderness in an amazingly short time. Below its surface are the skeletons of smashed vehicles and equipment bulldozed into the foundations of the road when there was not time to move them. At intervals along its path lie the ruins of hutted camps being slowly overgrown by the invading forest.

For three days we fled before a storm which threatened to overtake us and cut us off. Behind, whole sections of the

Highway were being washed away, but our Canadian army driver kept the big car's hood in front of the deluge and late on the third evening we rode into Dawson Creek and fine weather.

With typical enthusiasm Scotty McCleod had arranged an exhausting weekend program and also lifts in trucks for us all to Edmonton. This last section of the road journey, in great diesel monsters which rampaged along at sixty miles an hour, the drivers taking bends like Mille Miglia competitors, was an education in driving, and a wall of deathlike experience. I was glad to board the sedate train to Montreal.

I broke my journey at Ottawa, to report to the head of the U.K. staff. Our trouble-free and safe return was received almost thankfully. Now that we had proved ourselves fairly harmless, and success had lent respectability to our venture, an interview had been arranged for me with the U.K. High Commissioner, General Sir Archibald Nye. I found this brilliant soldier, who as Vice C.I.G.S. had been in the midst of the stuff of history in the last war, keen to hear of what we had done and pleased at our success. He was delighted that we had received some publicity in the press and on radio and television at a time when, because of the dollar barrier, the average Canadian saw or knew so little of British people. When he learned that I was sitting for the Staff College examination in the following February he spent the last ten minutes of the interview in giving me a good deal of considered advice on how to pass. The interview at an end, I left the room deeply impressed by his friendliness and the quiet, benign authority of his personality.

For thirteen long days we voyaged lazily through calm seas to England. Nasser and the Suez Canal troubles seemed utterly remote. When we arrived at Southampton we found

George Greenfield there to greet us with the news that he had
pushed us into the newspapers and onto "In Town Tonight."
He also produced an urgent message from the War Office
requiring us to report for an appearance on TV. Success indeed! On the other side of the port the remainder of the
Parachute Brigade was embarking for Cyprus.

The expedition split up with phenomenal speed at Water-
loo, its component members vanishing into the depths of
London. Later, Warwick and I confronted the microphone,
sandwiched between a girl parachutist and two stars advertising their latest film. Modestly we described the expedition in three minutes flat. The ten hectic days that followed were spent in attempting to put the aftermath of the
expedition into some order. I also visited the War Office to
find out if my next move would be to the Mediterranean,
but learned nothing.

After the adventure came the anticlimax and the letdown.
The elation of our homecoming spiraled away down to a
flat depression which reached its nadir as the four of us sat
in a cafe in Hyde Park dejectedly drinking tea from cracked
cups. Around us the shabby green tables and chairs, sticky
with spilled tea, and with their paint peeling, offended and
disgusted me. Not even the bright sun glinting on the grass
could dispel the dreariness of the place. I felt a strange contempt for the faceless crowds which hurried and eddied
about us. They did not know our other world. This was
theirs and I did not belong. Only the mountains seemed
real.

In that state of complete ignorance and uncertainty, which
in the Army one soon learns to shrug off with a dour fatalism,
Jeanne and I motored back to Germany. In the grey German
Barracks I reported for duty to my new O.C., David Morgan.
We spoke briefly about the expedition, and he gave me the
oracle's answer on the Middle East trouble: "It seems that

we are staying." He went on, in the next breath, to talk of more immediate things.

"Well, the exercise season is just about over and now we've got all these damned inspections coming off. There's the Adm inspection, the C.I.V.—I think we'll have to start drawing up a program. . . . I'm giving you transport and training, so would you let me have your plot on. . . ." I was back!

APPENDIX A

EQUIPMENT AND CLOTHING

EXPEDITION EQUIPMENT

2 Cine cameras
Cine film
  6,500 ft. Kodachrome
15 Rolls 35-mm film
  Agfacolor and Kodachrome
10 Rolls Kodak HP3
1 Bottle boot oil
12 Ration bags
24 Polythene bags
30 Paper bags
Cord and wire
4 Carrying frames
100 Route flags
2 Flashlights
10 Batteries
4 Spare bulbs
1 Vacuum flask
1 Sledge and harness
1 Sledge tarpaulin
1 Ground sheet
100 ft. hemp line
2 Snow shovels
1 Mirror
100 META tablets
Cleaning materials
15 Ration boxes
4 Karabiners

4 Line loops
1 Pr. crampons
6 Rock pitons
12 Ice pitons
2 Prismatic compasses
2 Protractors
3 Maps
1 Pr. binoculars
2 Map cases
6 Pencils
Stationery
2 Candle lanterns
2 Doz. boxes of matches
3 Doz. candles
Alarm clock
12 Small can openers
1 Spring balance (200 lb.)
6 Polythene bottles
1 Tent repair bag
1 Piton hammer
15 Spare tent pegs
1 Snow saw
Toilet paper
Quantity of sacking
6 Kit bags
2 Pr. goggles
4 Pr. snowshoes

2 100-ft. Nylon lines
2 H.A. nipples
8 Gals. kerosene
6 Thermometers
1 Barometer
80 Labels
3 Two-man tents

4 125-ft. Nylon ropes
3 Primus stoves
1 Funnel
3 Billies
1 Anemometer
2 Ice axes

NOTES: All our equipment, which was of normal design bought from London shops, proved highly satisfactory. The only exceptions were the War Department ice axes and snowshoes which were of inferior quality.

Snowshoes are essential on Alaskan glaciers and the long trail type would be the best choice.

The U.S. Akio, or plastic boat type sledge, was not suitable for the heavy loads we hauled. A ten- or eleven-foot Nansen sledge might have proved a better, although probably less durable, substitute.

With heavy and awkward loads packframes are superior to rucksacks or Everest carriers. Ours were army alloy wireless carriers of girder construction. Lugs were welded on, to which a waist band was fitted and each frame had a tump line, but this was not popular. One U.S. Army packboard was also used and was found to be not quite as good, for loads of sixty pounds and over, as the modified British frames.

PERSONAL CLOTHING AND EQUIPMENT

1 Pr. Himalayan boots
1 Pr. American rubber boots
1 Woolen vest
1 Rayon string vest
2 Thick shirts
3 Sweaters
1 Windproof suit
2 Pr. under trousers

1 Balaclava helmet
1 Hat
1 Scarf
2 Pr. windproof mitts
2 Pr. woolen gloves
1 Pr. silk gloves
2 Pr. goggles
1 Ice axe

2 Waist loops
2 Karabiners
1 Pr. tent boots
6 Pr. socks
1 Pr. boot insoles
1 Towel
Washing kit
Knife, fork, spoon
1 Deep plate
1 Mug
1 Water bottle

String
1 Sewing kit
1 Whistle
1 Clasp knife
2 Books
1 Diary
Writing materials
2 Pr. spare boot laces
1 Air mattress
1 Double sleeping bag
1 Pr. crampons

Other Clothing: Battle Dress or Service Dress with Web Belt or Sam Browne, together with Plain Clothes.

NOTES: Our clothing was again the normal mountaineering expedition wear. The American Super Thermo-Ply Oneida Rubber Boots were excellent for all types of work. With the addition of Vibram soles, quick-release lacing, and insoles they would probably be the answer to both extreme cold and high-altitude climbing. I was the only member of the party to use the Himalayan Boot and I soon reverted to the other pattern.

I wore a pair of gloves made of an American artificial fabric called Dynel. It is extremely warm and hard wearing and could be used successfully for sleeping mats or tent boots or made up into thick shirts or sweaters.

APPENDIX B

THE DIETARY INTAKE AND ACTIVITIES OF THE PARACHUTE BRIGADE ALASKA EXPEDITION [*]

By Dr. Donald Kinloch
of the Royal Infirmary, Glasgow
(*Medical Officer of the Expedition*)

THERE ARE few records of the calorie intake and energy expenditure of expeditions in the field. A trained physiologist is not usually available and, however desirable ancillary investigations may be, the chance of achieving the primary objective of the expedition must not be jeopardized. This is particularly so with mountaineering expeditions.

Throughout the six weeks during which the Parachute Brigade Alaska Expedition was in the mountains and entirely self-supporting, the food consumption and daily activities of the individual climbers were studied. An accurate assessment of the dietary intake was facilitated by the simplicity of the rationing system, the length of the study, and the reasonably close medical supervision throughout the entire period. By checking body-weights at intervals, it was possible to assess whether or not an individual was in approximate metabolic balance. As a rough guide to energy expenditure records were made, by a diary technique, of

[*] Reprinted by permission of the editor from the *British Journal of Nutrition*, 1959, 13, 85.

all daily activities. It was not possible to take a respirometer to make accurate measurements of the energy expenditure by estimating oxygen consumption. Not only would porterage have been a problem, but the inherent difficulties of an arduous climbing expedition precluded the use of such a method.

The members of the expedition were all trained parachutists and as such were of above-average fitness. Their selection was based primarily on their mountaineering experience. Details of physique are given in Table 1.

INVESTIGATION

Records. (The remainder of this paper on diet and activities are as in the reprint.)

EXPERIMENTAL

The Expedition

Composition: The members of the expedition were all trained parachutists and as such were of above-average fitness. Their selection was based primarily on their mountaineering experience. Details of physique are given in Table 1. Each member of the expedition was delegated specific tasks: the leader (J.M.) was responsible for all organization and day-to-day planning, and, in addition, collected specimens for a geological survey; the second-in-command (W.D.) was the accountant and meteorologist; the medical officer (D.K.) was responsible for health and ration administration; the fourth member of the party (D.P.) was the official expedition photographer and artist.

Itinerary: Exploration of Alaskan mountains presents not only the complexities of Arctic travel, but in addition

TABLE 1.

AGES, HEIGHTS, WEIGHTS, AND SURFACE AREAS OF THE CLIMBERS

	D.K.	J.M.	W.D.	D.P.
Age (years)	26	29	29	24
Height (cm)	176	175	185	171
Surface area (m²)	1.85	1.80	2.06	1.77
Body-weight (kg):				
Initially, 1st day	68.6	65.0	79.5	68.2
At end of period 1 (glacier), 10th day	69.2	65.5	78.6	65.0
At end of period 2 (climbing), 15th day	69.2	65.0	76.9	67.8
At end of period 3 (glacier), 22nd day	68.2	64.4	77.3	65.5
At end of period 4 (climbing), 32nd day	68.6	64.6	77.7	65.5
At end of periods 5–6 (glacier and climbing), 39th day	68.2	64.6	79.5	65.5
At end of period 7 (glacier), 41st day	69.7	64.6	77.7	65.9
Mean	68.8	64.6	78.2	66.4

the difficulties of Alpine climbing. Every peak is ice-capped and every valley over 2,000 feet in altitude is glaciated. As a result, any exploration party endeavoring to gain access to the mountains encounters considerable preliminary difficulty on the glaciers, which, because of Arctic weather conditions and steep gradients, are rapidly moving and consequently heavily crevassed.

It was at the foot of one of these unexplored glacier systems, the Traleika Glacier, that a U.S.A.A.F. helicopter set down the expedition, along with its 1,000 pounds (450 kilograms) of supplies and equipment. These had to be transported up some 20 miles of heavily crevassed glacier by backpacking and sledge-hauling; neither dog teams nor porters were available.

The altitude of the glacier traversed was between 5,000 and 7,000 feet (1,600 and 2,100 meters). From a base

camp on the glacier, four virgin peaks of heights between
11,000 feet (3,300 meters) and 13,000 feet (3,900 meters)
were climbed; the ascent of these mountains usually neces-
sitated one or two camps on the way to the summit, the
final assaults being launched from cols at a height of 10,000
feet (3,000 meters). Setting up the high camps was invariably a slow business; weaving a route through ice falls and
climbing steep ice slopes, often with step-cutting, while
heavily laden, was no easy task.

One of the great advantages of climbing in Alaska is that
there is continuous daylight in summer and the program
for the day is determined by the snow conditions and not by
the clock. The climate in Alaskan mountains is one of extremes. The temperatures range from 0°F (−18°C) at midnight to 80°F (27°C) at noon when the glacier basin greatly
intensifies the effects of the sun's rays. On the average, however, temperatures in the very early morning were between
20° and 25°F, so, whenever possible, all climbing and marching were done at this time. Because temperatures were below freezing, the danger from avalanches and the bridging
of crevasses was minimized and, in addition, sledge-hauling
and load-carrying were facilitated.

Fresh snow provided a further complication, but on only
six days was climbing actually prevented by heavy snowfall, although load-transporting was considerably hampered
on many occasions by several feet of soft snow on the glacier.

INVESTIGATION

Records: Each individual received daily a form for recording activity and food consumption. In order to overcome the difficulties caused by the constant daylight and
the complete irregularity of eating and sleeping times, the
form covered a "ration day"—from after breakfast till after

breakfast—these periods ranging from 12 to 30 hours. Exact times of all activities and meals were noted, and results were later converted to show the dietary intake and activity of individuals for 24-hour periods; these periods were taken from midday to midday, which often coincided with a "ration day."

Rations: There were four basic types of ration, all designed for the use of isolated Army units in the field, but equally suitable for any small mountaineering expedition.

A "compo" type of ration (Table 2), designed specially for the expedition, provided the bulk of the food supply. It was simple in composition and of low cost; the ratio of calorie value to bulk and gross weight was good, and a European type of diet was provided. The design permitted considerable ease in packing, transportation and distribution. Four variations, ration types A, B, C, and D, made the ration more acceptable over a long period. Most foods were tinned or dried and obtainable at any general provision store. Vacuum-packed foods were excluded on grounds of cost. The rations were packed in standard R.A.S.C. sleeve-type boxes, each having a gross weight of 35 pounds (16 kilograms) and containing two 8-man-day units. A daily ration of 26–30 ounces (730–840 grams) net of food per man was provided with a caloric value averaging 3,370 calories at a cost of 4s. 3d. (Table 3).

In addition there were for the whole expedition 60 pounds (27 kilograms) of luxury items. Part of these had to be used to eke out the normal rations for four days and some provided emergency pocket rations of fudge and glucose tablets for each climber. The remainder provided a daily supplement of 4 ounces (112 grams) of assorted foods per man. Luxury items were distributed, as far as possible, on demand, each individual receiving the same quantity; they

TABLE 2.

(A) CONTENTS OF A MAN-DAY RATION FROM A 2 × 8 MAN-DAY STANDARD RATION PACK AND A 4 MAN-DAY EMERGENCY RATION PACK AND (B) EXTRA LUXURY ITEMS FOR THE WHOLE EXPEDITION

A (ALL VALUES IN OUNCES)

	Type A	Type B	Type C	Type D	Emergency ration
Pemmican	2	—	—	—	—
Corned beef	—	3	—	—	—
Stewed steak	—	—	4	—	—
Luncheon meat	—	—	—	2	—
Sardines	1⅛	—	—	1⅛	—
Cheese	—	2	2		—
Porridge oats	3	—	3	3	1½
Grape-nuts	—	1¼	—	—	—
Nut pemmican	—	—	—	—	2
Soup	—	—	—	—	½
Mint cake (Kendal)	—	—	—	—	2
Cake (fruit)	2	—	—	2	—
Steamed pudding	—	2½	2½	—	—
Glucose tablets (Horlick's Energade)	—	—	—	—	¾
Orangeade powder (Army)	—	—	—	—	2
Sugar			4		4
Condensed milk			1½		—
Tea			¼		—
Butter			1⅞		—
Biscuits (Army)			3		—
Biscuits (sweet)			2		—
Chocolate			4		2
Sweets			2		—
Fudge (Horlick's)			—		2

B (EXCEPT SOUP, ALL VALUES IN POUNDS; TOTAL WEIGHT 60 POUNDS)

Soup	16 (packets)	Preserves (various)	2
Meat bars	1½	Fudge	2
Dried vegetable	1	Sugar	2
Dried potato	4	Vita-Wheat	8
Baked beans	4	Beverages (various)	6
Rice	2	Tablets (Horlick's and Ovaltine)	4
Nut pemmican	3	Peanut butter	2
Dried fruit	6	W.D. butter concentrate	3
Tinned fruit	6	Salt	2

TABLE 3.

PROTEIN, FAT, CARBOHYDRATE, AND CALORIE YIELD PER MAN PER DAY AND DAILY COST PER MAN OF THE RATIONS USED ON THE EXPEDITION *

Ration	No. of days used	Protein (grams)	Fat (grams)	Carbo-hydrate (grams)	Energy (calories)	Weight (grams)	Cost
Standard ration:							
Type A	12	60	150	480	3490	750	4s. 7d.
Type B	8	55	160	440	3370	770	4s. 3d.
Type C	6	60	175	470	3710	840	3s. 11d.
Type D	2	50	150	460	3350	750	3s. 10d.
Emergency	2	15	60	330	1920	470	2s. 6d.
Army "Snow" †	4	140	190	460	4170	980	>10s. 0d.
Army G.S. Mk. V †	5	98	140	550	3860	1230	>10s. 0d.

* The composition was calculated from the manufacturer's figures and the standard tables of the Ministry of Food (1951) based on those of the Medical Research Council: Accessory Food Factors Committee (1945).
† See below.

added considerable variety to the daily ration in the way of preserves, extra fruit and vegetables, biscuits and sweets, and a selection of beverages. There was a five-days' supply of Army 24-Hour Ration Packs G.S. Mk. V and a four-days' supply of Army 24-Hour Snow Rations (a fifth day's supply being consumed by a predatory raven). These rations were very convenient in use and were considered comparatively luxurious; they had the disadvantages of greater weight and expense, and the G.S. Mk. V Ration was considerably more bulky than the standard expedition ration. A two-day supply of small, lightweight emergency rations was also carried.

Food intake: As mentioned earlier, the simplicity of the rations greatly assisted the individual in recording his food consumption. On his form he would note the type of ration issued for the day, and any extra items consumed or left over; the extra items were usually chocolate, sweets, and biscuits, and the weights were therefore readily estimated.

A record was also kept of all fluid intake. Mugs were marked off in measures to assist estimation of fluid. Water was obtained from pools in the central moraine of the lower glacier but at the high camps snow or, where possible, ice was melted over paraffin pressure stoves or, occasionally, melted in a heat-absorbing container, e.g., a black plastic cape, laid out in the sun. As in any climbing expedition, a certain amount of artificiality must have occurred in providing for the fluid and calorie intake since each man was issued with his daily ration, which meant that supply was not necessarily related to demand. A man could either hand over his unwanted food to a communal pool or store more suitable items, such as sweets, until a later occasion. On the whole, however, each man tended to take what was put before him —not always eating merely on account of hunger or a good appetite, but eating for the sake of eating as is the wont of civilized races. This habit is particularly noticeable on an arduous mountaineering expedition where eating and sleeping are two of the main joys in life.

Physical activities: Each man noted on his form the time spent on different activities throughout the day; these activities were classified under the three main headings of sleeping (including resting within sleeping bags), minor activity (either within tents or around camp), and exertion (including climbing and marching).

The estimates of sleeping and resting were combined, since the true sleeping time was reduced on an average to about 50 per cent of the attempted sleeping time because of such factors as fatigue, altitude, overcrowded tents at high camps, and the extremes of heat and cold experienced during the usual afternoon and evening sleeping period.

Minor activity included all the incidental daily tasks of any expedition from dressing, cooking, and mending within tents to performing one's toilet, carrying water, pitching and striking camp, and photography around the campsite. All minor activity around the campsite, however, was restricted to a radius of some 10 yards because of the constantly present danger of hidden crevasses.

For climbing and marching a record was kept of terrain, distances, heights, and loads, in addition to timings; all rest periods of more than a minute or two, and halts for food, were deducted and included under minor activity.

A useful cross-check on timings was provided by the fact that, apart from minor activity, the whole party was almost invariably doing the same thing at any one time.

Body-weights: (Table 1.) Body-weights were recorded at intervals by means of a spring balance (0–100 kilograms) suspended from an ice axe, the subject sitting on a rope sling attached to the hook of the balance. No opportunity occurred to calibrate the balance accurately throughout its entire range, but comparison with two other weighing machines (of lever and spring type respectively) revealed a variation of less than 1 kilogram for the weights recorded.

RESULTS

Dietary Intake

The mean daily calorie intake and hours of activity are shown in Table 4.

The six weeks spent on the expedition are broken into seven periods according to whether the major activity was glacier marching or actual climbing. The mean calorie intake for each period is shown in Table 4, together with mean calorie intakes for all the days spent either marching on the glacier, climbing, or resting. The mean intakes for the whole period of the expedition are given in Table 7.

In Table 5 a further breakdown of the diet is shown giving the mean consumption of protein, fat, and cabohydrate for the various periods, and for further subdivided types of activity.

The calorie intake while climbing was considerably lower (3,495 calories) than that on the glacier (4,100 calories), save in the last climbing period, which was an 18-hour mountain ascent from a base camp on the glacier. Although exertion while climbing was always considerably more strenuous than that on glacier marches, the calorie intake was thought to be lower primarily because the weights to be carried, and hence the rations issued, were reduced to facilitate climbing under difficult conditions, as on steep ice slopes. Further contributing factors to the low calorie intake were the physical and mental fatigue after a strenu-

TABLE 4.
DAILY CALORIE INTAKE AND HOURS OF
ACTIVITY OF THE MEMBERS OF THE
EXPEDITION

Period	Day no.	Activity	Calorie intake (Cal.)	Hours spent daily in		
				Exertion	Sleep	Minor activities
1	1	Glacier	3825	3	9	12
	2	Glacier	3630	6	8	10
	3	Glacier	2850	4	9	11
	4	Glacier	3450	7	6½	10½
	5	Glacier	3920	7½	9	7½
	6	Glacier	3470	8½	3½	12
	7	Glacier	3465	5	10	9
	8	Glacier	3525	5	9	10
	9	Rest day	4120	—	11	13
	10	Rest day	4350	—	9	15
	Mean		3640	4½	8½	11
2	11	Climbing*	3240	11	2	11
	12	Climbing*	1080	3	9	12
	13	Climbing*	3795	8½	6½	9
	14	Rest day	3390	—	14	10
	15	Climbing*	3420	10	4	10
	Mean		2985	6½	7	10½
3	16	Glacier: rest day	4770	—	15	9
	17	Glacier†	4310	8	6	10
	18	Glacier	3620	7	8	9
	19	Glacier	3940	5½	6	12½
	20	Glacier	3390	5	8	11
	21	Glacier	3015	—	13	11
	22	Glacier	5000	3	7	14
	Mean		4010	4	9	11
4	23	Climbing*	4320	8	4	12
	24	Rest day	2600	—	12	12
	25	Climbing*	4865	6½	5	12½
	26	Rest day	3035	—	9	15
	27	Climbing	3500	4	12	8
	28	Rest day	4105	—	13	11
	29	Climbing	2670	7	11	6
	30	Climbing	3655	8	7	9
	31	Climbing	2585	7	9	8
	32	Climbing*	3800	9	8	7
	Mean		3515	5	9	10

| | | | Calorie intake (Cal.) | Hours spent daily in | | |
Period	Day no.	Activity		Exertion	Sleep	Minor activities
5	33	Glacier†	5440	5	7	12
	34	Glacier	5745	6	8	10
	35	Glacier	3820	8	7	9
	36	Glacier	3740	$6\frac{1}{2}$	8	$9\frac{1}{2}$
	37	Glacier	4855	$1\frac{1}{2}$	$11\frac{1}{2}$	11
	Mean		4720	$5\frac{1}{2}$	$8\frac{1}{4}$	$10\frac{1}{4}$
6	38	Climbing*	4390	$13\frac{1}{2}$	6	$4\frac{1}{2}$
	39	Climbing*	4105	$4\frac{1}{2}$	9	$10\frac{1}{2}$
	Mean		4250	9	$7\frac{1}{2}$	$7\frac{1}{2}$
7	40	Glacier	5875	11	4	9
	41	Glacier	4265	$12\frac{1}{2}$	5	$6\frac{1}{2}$
	Mean		5070	12	$4\frac{1}{2}$	$7\frac{1}{2}$

Loads carried: Usual load while climbing, under 10 lb. (4.5 kg). Usual load on glacier, 30–80 lb. (13–36 kg) with sledge-hauling 220–320 lb. (100–150 kg).

* Load while climbing, 30–70 lb. (13–32 kg).

† Load on glacier, under 10 lb. (4.5 kg).

ous day's climbing which reduced the desire both to cook and to eat food, sleep often being preferred.

The highest calorie intake was recorded on days spent traversing the glacier (4,100 calories) although it was almost identical to the mean intake for rest days on the glacier (4,065 calories). The over-all mean for rest days was reduced to 3,675 calories because some rest days were enforced by inclement weather at the camps at 10,000 feet where rations were short.

The highest calorie intake for any one day (5,875 calories) was on the final march down the glacier, during which the party, each man carrying a 90-pound (41-kilogram) pack, was on the move for 24 of the last 36 hours spent in the mountains, gorging themselves at their food depots en route, as they hastened to keep a date with a helicopter in the foothills.

TABLE 5.

MEAN DAILY DIETARY INTAKE AND HOURS OF ACTIVITY OF THE FOUR MEMBERS OF THE EXPEDITION FOR DIFFERENT PERIODS

		Individuals				Mean for the four men: Intake				Hours spent in		
Activity	*No. of days*	*D.K.* (*Cal.*)	*J.M.* (*Cal.*)	*W.D.* (*Cal.*)	*D.P.* (*Cal.*)	*Calories* (*Cal.*)	*Protein* (*g*)	*Fat* (*g*)	*Carbohydrate* (*g*)	*Exertion*	*Sleep*	*Minor activities*
Whole period	41	3940	3590	3860	3905	3825	73	163	517	$5\frac{1}{2}$	$8\frac{1}{4}$	$10\frac{1}{4}$
Days of glacier travel .	20	4265	3815	4105	4205	4100	75	179	545	$4\frac{1}{2}$	$7\frac{1}{2}$	$10\frac{1}{4}$
Days spent climbing . .	13	3530	3335	3590	3530	3495	70	144	480	$7\frac{3}{4}$	$7\frac{1}{4}$	9
Rest days	8	3805	3430	3700	3760	3675	74	151	504	0	12	12
Period 1, glacier	10	3755	3360	3685	3765	3640	66	158	478	$4\frac{1}{2}$	$8\frac{1}{2}$	11
Period 2, climbing	5	3000	2835	3055	3050	2985	55	132	396	$6\frac{1}{2}$	7	$10\frac{1}{2}$
Period 3, glacier	7	4230	3520	4095	4185	4010	72	169	534	4	9	11
Period 4, climbing	10	3610	3405	3535	3515	3515	76	143	481	5	9	10
Period 5, glacier	5	4805	4575	4800	4705	4720	80	205	638	$5\frac{1}{2}$	$8\frac{1}{4}$	$10\frac{1}{4}$
Period 6, climbing	2	4310	4065	4310	4310	4250	59	153	658	9	$7\frac{1}{2}$	$7\frac{1}{2}$
Period 7, glacier	2	5300	4805	4774	5300	5070	92	240	635	12	$4\frac{1}{2}$	$7\frac{1}{2}$
Days of activity	33	3975	3625	3900	3040	3860	73	165	520	$6\frac{3}{4}$	$7\frac{1}{2}$	$9\frac{3}{4}$
Days on glacier (including rest days) . .	24	4190	3780	4215	4215	4075	75	176	545	$5\frac{1}{4}$	$8\frac{1}{4}$	$10\frac{1}{2}$
Rest days on glacier . .	4	4150	3600	4245	4255	4065	87	171	544	0	12	12
Rest days over 9000 ft.	4	3460	3260	3155	3260	3285	61	131	463	0	12	12
Climbing over 9000 ft.	7	3153	3120	3225	3155	3165	77	128	424	$6\frac{1}{4}$	$8\frac{1}{2}$	$9\frac{1}{4}$
Days at over 9000 ft. . .	11	3265	3170	3200	3195	3205	72	130	439	4	$9\frac{3}{4}$	$10\frac{1}{4}$

An emergency bivouac after a mishap at the end of a difficult ice-fall ascent brought about the lowest daily calorie intake (1,080 calories) of the expedition as a result of a ration shortage and the general fatigue of the party.

The mean individual intakes throughout the expedition, over a period of 41 days, showed, on the whole, no great variation. Two members of the party (D.K. and D.P.) tended to feel the need for every morsel of food provided, and they had the highest intake (over 3,900 calories). The other two were more restrained, although the most heavily built individual (W.D.) had almost as high an intake (3,-860 calories). J.M., however, consistently and noticeably ate less (3,590 calories) than the others and frequently did not consume his entire ration.

The mean individual intakes of protein, fat, and carbohydrate showed only slight variations in quantity and proportions. There was no consistent alteration in proportions for any particular type of activity or with increased altitude.

Protein provided only 8 per cent of the total calorie intake, which is below the minimum of 11 per cent recommended by the British Medical Association: Committee on Nutrition (1950). The low protein intake was mainly due to the composition of the standard expedition ration; the desire for more meat was indeed felt by individuals and there was little adequate protein supplement in the luxury boxes. Another ounce (28 grams) of high-protein food per man per day in the basic ration would have been a most desirable addition.

The intake of vitamins and calcium also did not meet the recommended B.M.A. standards, as is shown in Table 6. An important contribution to this intake was made by the luxury items. However, a compound vitamin capsule was consumed daily and, besides providing adequate vitamins,

TABLE 6.

MEAN DAILY INTAKE PER MAN OF VITAMINS AND MINERALS OF THE FOUR MEMBERS OF THE EXPEDITION

	Standard rations	Standard rations and luxury items	Vitamin* capsule taken in addition	Recommended allowance†
Vitamin A (i.u.)	2517	4360	5000	2500
Thiamine (μg)	672	1200	3000	1600
Riboflavin (μg)	784	1500	3000	1800
Nicotinic acid (mg)	4.8	12	20	16
Ascorbic acid (mg)	1.5	13	75	20
Vitamin D (i.u.)	215	340	500	150
Calcium (mg)	420	500	—	800
Iron (mg)	27	28	—	12

* Vimagna, a compound vitamin capsule (Lederle Laboratories Ltd.).
† British Medical Association: Committee on Nutrition (1950), recommended allowance for a 4000-Cal. diet.

it had a marked psychological effect on individuals who felt they might be deprived of adequate nutrition.

Pemmican was the only item in the ration not normally consumed in a European diet; although well tolerated, it was received unenthusiastically, and meat bars would have been preferred. Dried soups were, whenever possible, added to the ration from the luxury boxes. These, with nutritive tablets such as Horlick's or Ovaltine tablets, would seem to be most acceptable for any expedition in Arctic or sub-Arctic climates. The generous daily rations of chocolate and butter were fully appreciated and between them provided over 1,000 calories per day.

The fluid intake varied little from one individual to another and averaged 4 pints (2.3 liters) daily; above 9,000 feet (1,700 meters) the mean dropped to 3-1/2 pints (2.0 liters). This amount was considerably less than the mean of

5–7 pints (2.8–4.0 liters) of fluid consumed daily by members of the Everest expedition (Pugh, 1954).

ENERGY EXPENDITURE AND DAILY ACTIVITY

There was considerable variation in the times and duration of the various activities from day to day, as shown in Table 4. It was due to the 24 hours of daylight, the only factors restricting activity being the snow and weather conditions. All periods of time spent in the various activities were essentially the same for each member of the expedition, apart from differences of 1–2 hours on only three occasions. The heavily crevassed glaciers required that the whole party be roped together on all occasions while on the move.

On the glacier, marching time varied from 1 to 18 hours at any one stretch and climbing time from 3 to 18 hours.

Hours of sleep (which included hours spent awake in sleeping bags) varied from 2 on a climbing day to 15 on a rest day. The mean daily sleeping time for the expedition was 8-1/4 hours, which agrees with the observations of Lewis and Masterton (1957) on the North Greenland expedition that, despite the irregularity of sleep, the over-all mean approximated to the time normally spent asleep in civilization.

Loads carried by individuals varied widely. On the glacier, in the process of relaying supplies, the average load was between 30 and 40 pounds (13–18 kilograms) backpacked, with limits of 20–90 pounds (9–41 kilograms); in addition three men were usually sledge-hauling, while the fourth probed for crevasses. On the actual summit assaults, under 10 pounds (4.5 kilograms) were carried, but on the ascent to the high camps the loads were 50–70 pounds (22–32 kilograms). It had been hoped, with an accurate note of loads, heights, and distances for each individual, to make some estimate of energy expenditure and to draw a comparison with daily food consumption. Such an estimate would, however, be almost entirely guesswork owing to the wide variety of conditions encountered, ranging from simple marching to the ascent of ice falls and the extraction of men from crevasses. Therefore only the over-all times spent by the party in the three main activities—climbing and marching, minor duties, and sleeping—have been tabulated (Tables 4 and 5).

HEALTH

Throughout the expedition health was excellent. The only demands made on the medicine chest were for sleeping tablets and Elastoplast. Body-weights, as shown in Table 1, remained remarkably constant and at the finish the whole party felt very fit. The most exhausting factors, of which everyone was glad to be free, were the 24 hours of daylight and the six weeks of pent-up nervous tension resulting from the uncertainties of mountaineering and living constantly amid crevasse-ridden glaciers.

DISCUSSION

The provisioning of mountaineering and other expeditions in the field is still very arbitrary and empirical. However, renewed interest in recent years in the physiology of nutrition and a spate of postwar expeditions of exploration have led to a steadily increasing accumulation of information on the subject.

The longest period for which the calorie intake of a mountaineering expedition has been recorded is the 18 days during the approach march of the 1952 Himalayan expedition to Cho Oyu (Pugh, 1953) and for further periods on the same expedition of up to 10 days at an altitude of over 15,-

ooo feet (4,500 meters). Calorie expenditure for these periods was simultaneously estimated (Table 7).

It is inevitable that any estimate of energy expenditure by indirect calorimetry and diary technique while climbing under widely varying conditions can only be very approximate. Indeed, it has been found that the energy expenditure of the same individual climbing under the same set of conditions can vary up to 20 per cent on different occasions (Durnin, 1955).

On the successful 1953 Everest expedition, an approximate estimate of food consumption was made for the various stages of the approach march and assault; no record, however, was kept of food wasted, save by Ward who, at an altitude of over 21,000 feet (6,300 meters), recorded exactly over a period of two days the food consumed by himself and his companion, an intake of 2,600 calories per man per day (Pugh, 1954). Shipton (1938), on the 1935 Everest expedition, estimated the calorie intake of the climbers at an altitude between 17,000 feet (5,100 meters) and 21,000 feet (6,300 meters) to be approximately 2,000 calories. During glacier exploration on the 1954 North Greenland expedition, estimates were made of the food intake and energy expenditure of two sledding parties (Masterton, Lewis, and Widdowson, 1957). Each party consisted of two men, and estimates were made over periods of 10 and 19 days, respectively. The mean calorie intake was 4,770 calories per man per day. The mean daily energy expenditure was calculated to be 5,240 calories per man, but direct energy measurements were made of the basal metabolic rates only. Estimates at their base camp, over two periods totaling 11-14 days, showed a mean daily calorie intake of 3,910 calories and a calculated expenditure of 3,580 calories; no heavy work was done, but the environmental temperatures were constantly below 0°C. Similar studies have recently been

TABLE 7.

COMPARISON OF THE DAILY DIETARY INTAKE AND ENERGY EXPENDITURE OF MEN ON VARIOUS EXPEDITIONS AND IN TWO ACTIVE OCCUPATIONS

				Dietary intake				Type of activity		
Expedition or occupation	*Conditions*	*Length of study (days)*	*Estimated energy expenditure (Cal.)*	*Energy (Cal.)*	*Protein (g)*	*Fat (g)*	*Carbohydrate (g)*	*Work (h)*	*Minor activities (h)*	*Rest (h)*
Alaska	Whole period	41	—	3825	72	162	515	5½	10¼	8¼
Cho Oyu,* 1952	Approach march	18	4370	4270	108	110	713	5	2	17
	At 15,000 ft.	4	3220	3625	64	80	640	2	4	18
	Over 19,000 ft.	9	3960	3190	42	71	596	4	0	20
	At 20,000 ft.	9	—	3150	45	104	547	2	4	18
Everest,† 1953	Approach march	26	—	4328	110	231	453	—	—	—
	Base 18,000 ft.	—	—	3786	81	190	437	—	—	—
	Over 20,000 ft.	—	—	3869	75	184	478	—	—	—
	Assault	—	—	3208	46	54	638	—	—	—
Antarctic‡ (Scott in 1912)	Sledging	—	—	3975	85	125	690	—	—	—
North Greenland §	At base	11–14	3580	3910	126	163	447	4½	11½	8
	Sledging	10–19	5240	4770	117	292	418	6½	8¾	8¾
British Army cadets ‖	—	14	3420	3430	99	123	488	4ª	11½ª	8½ª
Coal miners**	—	7	3660	4030	121	190	500	6¾	9½	7¾

* Pugh (1953).
† Pugh (1954).
‡ Bartram (1954).
§ Masterton *et al.* (1957).
‖ Edholm *et al.* (1955).
ª Approximate values only.
** Garry *et al.* (1955).

carried out on the Commonwealth Antarctic Expedition. Welch, Mann, Insull, Friedemann, Buskirk, Kreide, Brebbia, Morana, and Daniels (1955) studied the calorie balance of eight United States soldiers during a 12-day period of bivouacking (meals being eaten indoors) at temperatures below −25°F (−32°C). Each day 5 hours of travel over snow was done with sledge-hauling and load-carrying. The maximum individual calorie requirement, based on food intake and corrected for weight loss, was estimated to be 4,260 calories.

After studies of 26 U.S. soldiers over a period of three weeks, Welch, Levy, Consolaxio, Buskirk, and Dee (1957) recommended a maximum calorie intake of 4,500 calories per day for men in an Arctic environment. They also stated that, provided a man is properly clothed, his calorie requirements appear to be proportional to the work he is doing and not to the temperature of his environment, although low temperatures will of themselves encourage activity.

As our Alaskan expedition studies lasted for six weeks, it was possible to eliminate many of the inaccuracies that occur in estimating calorie intake over shorter periods. Although it was not possible to measure the exact energy expenditure, the fact that there was no rapid gain or loss of weight by any member of the party suggests that over the whole period of the expedition each individual was in calorie balance, but not necessarily in daily balance. This balance implies that the calorie intake was adequate.

It may be seen from Table 7 that the calorie intake during the approach to the mountains was lower than that of other expeditions; even between 9,000 feet (1,700 meters) and 13,000 feet (3,900 meters) in Alaska, the intake was as low or lower than the Cho Oyu and Everest estimates at over 20,000 feet (6,300 meters). The calorie intake for the latter expeditions, however, was estimated from the rations issued, but these were not necessarily wholly consumed. The Alaskan estimate of calorie requirements was also considerably lower than that of Masterton *et al.* (1957) for the North Greenland sledding parties, although there was not a great difference in the time spent in the major activities. It would also seem doubtful whether energy expenditure of the order suggested by Durnin (1955) was ever reached. He calculated an expenditure of 5,900–7,000 calories for a 7-hour ascent and 3-hour descent with a load. The longest climb in Alaska involved 11-hour ascent and 7-hour descent with 30-pound (13-kilogram) loads.

It is of interest to speculate how much the availability of food is in itself a key factor in determining how much food is consumed from day to day of an expedition. As the four-man Alaskan expedition had to transport all its own supplies without the assistance of porters or dog teams, all loads were cut to the absolute minimum, thus artificially creating a limited value for the possible food intake. However, the entire party was of the opinion that on most occasions the over-all diet was adequate, if not generous, even if individual taste was not always catered for. In what way the sensations of appetite and hunger are related to energy expenditure is uncertain, but on the Alaskan expedition these sensations were, in the main, subordinated to necessity and satisfied only when food supplies would permit. Calorie balance was not achieved by the satisfying of appetite, but artificially by the distribution of rations.

All four climbers performed almost identical activities throughout the six weeks, and individual variation in calorie intake must therefore be accounted for by differences in physique and skill and hence the rate of energy expenditure. W.D., the most heavily built, did not appear to consume the greatest amount of food, although his intake differed little from that of D.K. and D.P. On the other hand,

J.M., the lightest in weight, consistently had an intake of between 100 and 400 calories below that of the others. This finding suggests that the dietary intake of W.D. and J.M. was adequate and provides further grounds for supposing that the intake of the whole party was probably adequate.

It is desirable in any expedition in the field that rations should conform to certain specifications, providing adequate nutrition with as little expense, weight, and bulk as possible. That these criteria are not fulfilled on many expeditions is often very noticeable. The proportion by weight of food to other equipment is always considerable, and in the Alaskan expedition food comprised one-half of the total weight; yet rations had been cut to a minimum with only a very small reserve to provide for unexpected contingencies.

After careful consideration of the desirable features of the ration and of the environment in which it is to be used, a compromise may have to be made in deciding its composition. On a climbing expedition it is necessary to provide the largest meal at the end of the day; breakfast must be speedily cooked and it must be possible to consume the snack lunch en route without cooking.

Table 8 compares the rations used on various expeditions and in the British Army. It is suggested that the standard expedition ration (types A, B, C, and D) with certain modifications, especially in the protein content, and supplemented by a few luxury items, fulfills the requirements for provisioning an expedition in the field. It compares very favorably with rations used on other expeditions and would be suitable for any other intended mountaineering expedition or for isolated units of the Armed Forces in the field, after suitable instruction in its use. This ration would overcome the major difficulties of cost, bulk, and handling in the field.

TABLE 8.
COMPARISON OF VARIOUS EXPEDITION AND ARMY RATIONS

		Weight (kg)	Gross volume (ml)	Gross weight (g)	Net weight (g)	Cost	Energy (Cal.)	Protein (g)	Fat (g)	Carbo-hydrate (g)
Alaska	Standard Sixteen man-day	15.7	1860	990	850	4s. 3d.	3370	60	160	465
	Emergency Eight man-day	3.4	1410	480	480	2s. 6d.	1920	15	60	330
British Army [*]	"Snow" One man-day	1.1	2130	1130	960	10s. 0d.	4140	141	191	464
	G.S. Mk. V One man-day	1.6	3210	1580	1300	10s. 0d.	3886	100	140	550
	"Compo" Ten man-day	18.9	2850	1890	1160	6s. 2d.	4100	129	198	448
Everest [†]	Assault One man-day	1.8	—	1810	1580	—	3208	46	54	638
	"Compo" Fourteen man-day	20.2	—	1440	—	4s. 6d.	4800	—	—	—
Antarctic (Scott in 1912) [‡]	Sledging Bulk	—	—	—	960	—	3975	85	125	690
North Greenland [§]	Sledging Bulk	—	—	—	760	—	4164	99	278	310
Kanchenjunga [‖]	Low altitude Nine man-day	22.5	—	2490	—	—	—	—	—	—
	High altitude Ten man-day	16.6	—	1660	—	—	—	—	—	—

[*] Smith (1954).
[†] Pugh (1954).
[‡] Bartram (1954).
[§] Masterton et al. (1957).
[‖] Evans (1956).

SUMMARY

1. Records were made of the individual calorie intakes of a four-man Alaskan mountaineering expedition over a period of six weeks. The mean intake for the whole period was found to be 3,825 calories daily.

2. The daily activities of the expedition are described. The mean time spent daily in major physical activities was 5-1/2 hours, in minor activities 10-1/2 hours, and in resting 8 hours. These times are compared with those of other expeditions and of two active occupations.

3. It is concluded that, as body-weights remained fairly constant, the four men were in approximate calorie balance, and that for the period of the expedition calorie intake provided an estimate of energy expenditure.

4. The principles of provisioning a small expedition in the field are outlined, and a suitable ration is described.

5. The dietary intake and energy expenditure for various expeditions in the field are compared.

I should like to thank Captain E. J. E. Mills, the leader of the expedition, and my two other climbing colleagues, for their cooperation and tolerance; I am also most grateful to Professor R. C. Garry and Dr. J. V. G. A. Durnin of the Institute of Physiology, Glasgow University, for much helpful advice and encouragement.

REFERENCES

Bartram, J. C. L. (1954), *Proc. Nutr. Soc.*, 13, 69.
British Medical Association: Committee on Nutrition (1950), *Report of the Committee on Nutrition*, London: British Medical Association.
Durnin, J. V. G. A. (1955), *T. Physiol.*, 128, 294.
Edholm, O. G., Fletcher, J. G., Widdowson, E. M., and McCance, R. A. (1955), *Brit. J. Nutr.*, 9, 286.

Evans, C. E. (1956), *Kangchenjunga: The Untrodden Peak*, Appendix B, by G. C. Band, London: Hodder and Stoughton.

Garry, R. D., Passmore, R., Warnock, G. M., and Durnin, J. V. G. A. (1955), *Spec. Rep. Ser. Med. Res. Coun., Lond.*, no. 289.

Lewis, H. E., and Masterton, J. P. (1957), *Lancet*, 272, 1262.

Masterton, J. P., Lewis, H. E., and Widdowson, E. M. (1957), *Brit. J. Nutr.*, 11, 346.

Medical Research Council: Accessory Food Factors Committee (1945), *M.R.C. (War) Memor.*, no. 14.

Mills, E. J. E. (1957), *Alpine J.*, 62, 121.

Ministry of Food (1951), Private communication.

Pugh, L. G. C. (1953), *Food Consumption and Energy Balance at Various Altitudes*, London: Allen and Unwin.

Pugh, L. G. C. (1954), *Proc. Nutr. Soc.*, 13, 60.

Shipton, E. (1938), *Chem. & Ind.*, 57, 1231.

Smith, H. G. (1954), *Proc. Nutr. Soc.*, 13, 45.

Welch, B. E., Mann, J. B., Insull, W., Friedemann, T. E., Buskirk, E. R., Kreide, M., Brebbia, R., Morana, N., and Daniels, F. (1955), *U.S. Army Med. Nutr. Lab. Rep.*, no. 173.

Welch, B. E., Levy, L. M., Consolazio, C. F., Buskirk, E. R., and Dee, T. E. (1957), *U.S. Army Med. Nutr. Lab. Rep.*, no. 202.

APPENDIX C

A NOTE ON THE GEOLOGICAL COLLECTION
MADE BY THE EXPEDITION

THE ROCK SPECIMENS collected by the expedition were later sent to Dr. Bradford Washburn, who subsequently passed them on to the United States Geological Survey. Here they were incorporated into a reference collection of similar material, contributed mainly by Dr. Washburn from his earlier expeditions to Mount McKinley.

Mr. Clyde Wahrhaftig, after a study of the collection in 1950, concluded that . . .

Most of the high and rugged mountains appear to be granitic. An oval granite batholith, 18 miles long and 14 miles wide, includes most of Mount McKinley and all of Mount Hunter; this batholith is the largest of several in the area. The granitic rocks intruded tightly folded metamorphosed sedimentary rocks of Paleozic and early Mesozoic age. North-dipping volcanic rocks of the Cretaceous Cantwell formation flank the range on the north and are overlain by Tertiary Nenana gravel, which dips north along the border of the range. Parts of the Muldrow, Peters and Foraker glaciers follow a zone of weak rocks along a major fault. . . .

Mr. Donald Eberlein, Chief of the Alaskan Geology Branch, in answer to a query from the author, had this to say about the expedition collection:

. . . the Traleika specimens have not received more than cursory megascopic examination and we have prepared no report on their geological implications. The specimens are almost all mildly metamorphosed sedimentary rocks, probably of Paleozoic or Mesozoic age. However, no fossils were detected during our cursory study. I regret that other commitments make it impossible for us to do more with this material at the present time.

APPENDIX D
GLACIOLOGY

THE TRALEIKA glacier system was more than just the scene of our activities in Alaska, it was also our main highway through the mountains. During the course of those six weeks it became to us a familiar, malignant and dangerous opponent. It gave us no respite; at no time could we move more than a few feet without being roped together, each man protecting the other. It exacted a toll on our nerves, our time and nearly our lives. In the end it almost trapped us.

We knew that conditions on the Traleika were exceptional and that the ice was moving at a phenomenal rate, but we could only guess at the reasons. We concluded that the probable cause was earthquake or unusual weather.

But it remained a mystery until I received a letter in December, 1958 from Mr. Austin S. Post. He wrote:

> I write regarding obtaining information and if possible, photographs of the Muldrow Glacier, Alaska, which you observed while acting as leader of the Parachute Brigade Alaska Expedition in the Spring of 1956.
> . . . As field leader of the 1957 IGY Project 4.11 mapping selected Alaskan glaciers, I had the good fortune to observe and photograph the remarkable changes which took place in this glacier and am now gathering material for a descriptive report of these changes, to be published by the American Geographical Society of New York.
> The observations which you reported in the 1957 American Alpine Journal were of great interest as it seems evident that

your party actually observed the beginning of the movement which displaced surface features of the glacier as much as four miles down-valley and lowered the surface of the ice in the upper Muldrow and Traleika Glacier several hundred feet. . . ."

I answered his questions, sent photographs and added a few other observations. When he replied I was extremely interested to note that he was of the opinion that ". . . you are the first to have witnessed the beginnings of one of these rare glacier 'floods'. . . ."

Mr. Post's paper was published in the *Journal of Geophysical Research* in November, 1960. By kind permission of the author and editor of the *Journal,* the relevant extracts are reproduced below.

THE EXCEPTIONAL ADVANCE
OF THE MULDROW, BLACK RAPIDS,
AND SUSITNA GLACIERS
Austin S. Post

INTRODUCTION

In the winter of 1956–1957, the Muldrow Glacier, after many years of quiescence and slow retreat, suddenly and unexpectedly made a spectacular advance, with ice movements down the glacier amounting to 6.6 km (4.1 mi) taking place in a few months. A similar short-lived movement was witnessed in the Black Rapids Glacier in 1936–1937, and in 1952 or 1953 the Susitna Glacier made a like movement.

These advances apparently are not a normal reaction to climatic changes and may have significance to our understanding of the mechanism of glacier flow;

All these glaciers are located in the Alaska Range in central Alaska. . . .

MULDROW GLACIER

This glacier is located on the northern slope of the Alaska Range in Mt. McKinley National Park. Heading in the summit snows of Mt. McKinley, 6193 meters (20,320 feet), North America's highest peak, the glacier, about 63 kilometers (39 miles) in length, descends abruptly to an elevation of about 2000 meters (6600 feet), then more gradually to its terminus at 762 meters (2500 feet). It is joined by its largest tributary, the Traleika, at an elevation of 1737 meters (5700 feet) and by another major branch, the Brooks Glacier, at an elevation of 1646 meters (5400 feet). Below the junction of the Traleika the glacier is quite uniform in gradient and width, which averages 2½ kilometers (1½ miles). The upper portion of the glacier flows in a northeasterly direction for a distance of 42 kilometers (26 miles). Here an abrupt 90° angle occurs and from this point the glacier trends northwesterly to the terminus. . . .

Conditions before Advance. For a period of at least 50 years the lower portion of the glacier has been wasting away with little movement taking place. Photographs taken in 1916 (Griffen) show debris-laden ice in the terminal area. Others taken since 1950 indicate that vertical wastage of as much as 200 meters (660 feet) has occurred during this period. Aerial views in 1936 (Washburn) of that portion of the glacier above the bend showed conditions essentially similar to those in 1952. At that time the glacier above the bend was characterized by lanes of rather smooth, uncrevassed ice and large, irregular moraines. Photographs taken from McGonagall Pass near the juncture of the Traleika and Muldrow in 1916 (Capps) and 1956 (Mills) show little change.

Early Phases of Advance. Although no one actually seems to have seen the beginning of the advance of the glacier,

personal observations and photographs kindly furnished to
the author by various persons who had been in the vicinity
in 1956 have brought out certain pertinent facts. Photographs by Viereck taken near the right-angle turn in the
lower glacier on July 16 show that below this point the
glacier was almost unchanged from former years. Views
up-glacier from the same point disclose notable shearing in
the form of crevassed and broken ice, particularly along the
northern margins several kilometers farther up the valley,
and what may be a wave of advancing ice extending completely across the glacier at a greater distance. In the immediate vicinity of the right-angle bend, the ice, although
not seriously disturbed, shows some marginal crevassing and
a convex profile, both of which are indications of activity.
Mills (private communication), leader of a mountain-climb-
ing party on the Traleika Glacier that year, definitely witnessed early phases of the actual movement. By his descrip-
tion, the Traleika Glacier was badly crevassed when the
group ascended that branch of the Muldrow in late May,
1956, and had become almost impassable by July 6. About
6 kilometers (4 miles) up the Traleika the surface level had
dropped an estimated 15 meters (50 feet) in this 6-week
interval. During this same period, the Muldrow Glacier
above its confluence with the Traleika had remained almost
unchanged.

It appears that extensive down-valley movements were
lowering the ice surface of the upper Traleika before July
6 and that the effects of such movements were just beginning to be manifest on July 16 at the right-angle bend 32
kilometers (20 miles) down the glacier.

Early in the spring of 1957, National Park officials first
noted that the lower glacier had advanced and many reports
followed describing the glacier as totally changed, including
several excited tales of the upper glacier having "collapsed,"

or "fallen in." This area was visited by several interested scientists: Péwé (1957) and Millett (unpublished manuscript, 1960); both reported their observations. In July the author made several aerial photo-reconnaissance flights over the area. In September the U.S. Navy obtained excellent aerial photographs.

As very little change took place after detailed observations were begun in June 1957, practically all the movement of ice in the glacier below the 90° bend took place in a period not exceeding 9 months.

Nature of Changes. Lower glacier. Views from the Denali Highway in 1957 disclosed that the lower glacier had been completely transformed since last observed in the fall of 1956. Where formerly the glacier had been a hardly recognizable moraine-covered mass almost concealed behind massive lateral moraines, fantastically broken *séracs* of blue ice now rose conspicuously. Closer examination disclosed that the ice advancing down-glacier had overridden and incorporated much of the nearly stagnant lower portion of the glacier but did not completely cover all of an area, of relic, ablation-moraine-covered ice dating from an older advance, judged from vegetational development to be nearly one hundred years old or even older (Viereck private communication). On the eastern side of the advancing glacier this brush-covered ice was compressed and pushed into large ridge-like "rolls." Margins of the glacier, formerly concave below the lateral moraines, now rose vertically 50 meters (160 feet) or more above the point of contact with the moraine, in most places towering high above its crest. This condition was present as far up-valley as the right-angle bend. . . . Streams from bordering mountains which formerly had drained through notches in the lateral moraine were dammed by the glacier and had formed lakes from which the water now escaped through old channels between the moraines and mountain slopes.

Middle portion of the glacier. Above the right-angle bend the rise of the surface of the glacier became progressively less pronounced and was negligible [5 kilometers (3 miles) above the right-angle turn.] For 25 kilometers (16 miles) beyond this point the surface was lower than before. . . . This lowering of the ice surface was present in all three major tributaries but was most pronounced in the upper trunk glacier and especially noticeable on the Traleika, which furnished the major portion of the ice involved in the advance. Movement of this tributary amounted to nearly 5.5 kilometers (3.4 miles) against 1.8 kilometers (1.1 miles) for the Brooks and 2 kilometers (1.2 miles) for the upper Muldrow. Most of the smaller, steeply descending tributaries had been greatly altered by this lowering of the main glacier's surface. The least affected were left hanging, their point of contact with the main glacier being marked by a sheer ice cliff as much as 61 meters (200 feet) high. The majority of these branches, however, had made large movements, and their formerly rather smooth surfaces had become steep cascades of shattered ice blocks.

Hanging "stranded" lateral moraines, ice fringes, and sheared-off lateral tributaries clearly indicate that the changes in this portion of the glacier were due almost entirely to a down-valley shift of the ice accompanied by a pronounced lowering of the glacier surface of as much as 61 meters (200 feet), or more. Sheared marginal remnants of ice, which in places appeared to have been thrust down-valley slightly before being left stranded by the lowering of the main glacier surface, suggest that the down-valley motion may have begun before the lowering.

The movement throughout the affected portion of the

glacier appears to have taken place in such a way that, although crevassed and broken into a fantastic mass of ice pinnacles, the main surface features consisting of medial moraines and avalanche debris remained clearly recognizable. One feature noted was that large areas of heavily debris-encumbered ice frequently remained at a higher level than the adjoining clean ice. The medial moraine extending from the juncture of the Muldrow and Traleika glaciers was a notable example of this, rising above the clean ice on either side almost vertically approximately 30 meters (100 feet), and forming a weirdly pinnacled, continuous wall for a distance of several kilometers.

Upper glacier. Where the larger tributaries become narrow and the gradient steepens near the head of the main valleys, the amount of lowering of the ice surface rapidly diminished. Above such points, including at least three quarters of the accumulation area of the glacier, no discernible change of surface levels took place.

Areas and Volume of Ice, Muldrow Advance. The 1957 firn limit occurred at about 2100 meters (7000 feet) above sea level and is considered to be about the maximum altitude the snowline rises on the glacier. . . .

Although the Muldrow Glacier covers approximately 393 square kilometers (152 square miles), the portion of the glacier affected by the advance was only about 167 square kilometers (64 square miles). Of this, 67 square kilometers (26 square miles) is . . . the area into which ice advanced, and 100 square kilometers (38 square miles) is the area in which loss of volume occurred. The loss of ice from the upper glacier and the gain by the lower glacier appears to be equal within the accuracy of available data. If an average surface lowering [of the upper glacier] of 45 meters (150

feet) is assumed, probably a minimum figure, the net exchange of ice from the upper to the lower glacier is calculated to be about 3.3 kilometers (0.8 miles). . . .

[The Black Rapids and the Susitna Glacier are then briefly
discussed.]

CONCLUSIONS

It has definitely been determined by examination of aerial
photographs and by personal observation that all the above
advances took place without contemporary movement of any
other glacier in the immediate vicinity.

Unusual Surface Features. The glaciers discussed above have
similar, although unusual, medial moraine patterns. These
consist of large bulb-like loops in the moraines which frequently extend almost from one side of the glacier to the
other. Nearly identical loops may be seen to repeat at intervals. Somewhat similar moraine patterns are found on a
very few other valley glaciers in Alaska, one being the West
Fork Chulitna. These moraine loops are probably caused by
intrusion of fast moving tributaries into the slower main
stream. The moraine loops are displaced down the valley by
advances of the trunk glacier. When movement of the trunk
glacier ceases, new ice bulbs are formed by the tributaries.
Aerial photographs (USAF and USGS) of the Black Rapids
Glacier in different years show deformation of this nature
taking place.

Significant Aspects. The glaciers covered in this report have
a number of features in common:

1. All have a fairly long, narrow main stem of relatively
low gradient (slope in the middle reach averaging about
30 meters/kilometers (120 feet/miles). All but the Yanert,

which has one, have three or more major tributary valley glaciers. Normally a reach 8 kilometers (5 miles) or more in length at the terminus is virtually stagnant and covered with debris.

2. Each advance, with the possible exception of that of the Yanert, of which little is know, was preceded by a long period (at least several decades) of inactivity in which the glacier was very inactive and thinning in its terminal regions.

3. As a result of the advance, the surface level in the middle reaches of the trunk and tributaries is lowered. The surface in the terminal area rises, and active ice overrides stagnant, debris-covered ice, but no net change in mass occurs. The surface changes in elevation may amount to 60 meters (200 feet) or more.

4. Surface features are displaced down-glacier by several kilometers but otherwise are little distorted by the advance.

5. Similar advances apparently have occurred in the past, and, in some cases at least, this may be a periodically recurring phenomenon.

Possible Causes. Glaciers are known to be very sensitive to climatic variations, so it is only natural to look first to this as the direct cause of these advances. Attempts to correlate the recent glacial history at the Black Rapids Glacier with other glaciers (Péwé 1953) imply acceptance of the climatic variations as the direct cause of the advance of this glacier. However, the advance of glaciers in the Yakutat Bay area in the very early 1900's was ascribed to abnormal avalanching of snow due to earthquakes (Tarr and Martin, 1914), an idea which has gained widespread acceptance. The possibility that a cycle of advance may be caused directly by wastage of a glacier was mentioned by Forel and Richter in the nineteenth century (Russell, 1899) and has been reported re-

cently (Streiff-Becker, 1957; Desio, 1954), but apparently it
has not been accepted generally by workers in the field of
glacier dynamics.

Climatic variation. No records have been kept which directly
indicate weather conditions on the Muldrow or other glaciers
described in this report. The general climatic pattern, however, is indicated from records kept since 1930 at McKinley
Park Station. . . . From these, no clear indication of any
general climatic change favoring glacier growth is apparent.

Despite this, the possibility of very local increases in snow
accumulation must be considered. It will be noted that:

  1. Contiguous glaciers (Susitna and Black Rapids firn) did
not behave similarly at the same time. In fact, the change
revealed by extensive crevassing at the head of Susitna
Glacier in 1954 was remarkable. The crevassing began only a
few hundred meters from a point in common firn from which
similar crevassing due to ice moving in the opposite direction
occurred during the Black Rapids advance in 1937. During
this interval a complete reversal of the dynamic condition of
the two glaciers took place.

  2. Glaciers in the Alaska Range advanced at widely different intervals in time. Advances cycled completely in a matter
of months; therefore these would not seem to be delayed
responses to a suitable general climatic variation.

  3. In at least one known case (Muldrow), the amount of
ice in the terminal advance equaled the amount of ice de-
pleted in upper reaches without any corresponding "refilling"
of the accumulation basin.

There was no discernible net addition of mass to the glacier.
Indications are that the Black Rapids and Susitna advances
were essentially the same as that of the Muldrow. Therefore,
even if a localized, sporadic distribution of climatic changes
had occurred, it could not have done more than act as a
trigger.

Earthquakes. All these glaciers occupy valleys which are believed to follow a major fault line. With but few exceptions, other glaciers situated farther east and farther west and occupying portions of this same fault system show at least some erratic surface features, while on nearby glaciers in valleys not associated with the fault such features generally are absent.

The advance of the Muldrow was not the result of ice being dislodged from surrounding mountains, because the steeper, upper portions of the glacier were unaffected and no extensive recent avalanching was observed anywhere in the basin.

[Between 1904 and 1956 there were eighteen recorded earthquakes in this part of the Alaska Range, five between March 2 and August 27, 1956.] . . . No direct relationship between these shocks and the various glacier advances is evident, although the earthquake of March 2, 1956, centering 50 kilometers (30 miles northeast of the Muldrow, or the March 30 shock for which no epicenter was plotted, should be considered as possible triggering mechanisms.

The possibility that earthquakes forming a shock wave within a glacier would result in a catastrophic advance has been proposed by A. E. Harrison (private communication).

No earthquakes have been recorded which show any relationship to the Black Rapids, Susitna, and Yanert advances. Moffit (1942) stated without elaboration that earthquakes did occur in the vicinity of the Black Rapids in 1936 and 1937. The fact that nearly all the glaciers in the Alaska Range which display erratic flow characteristics are located along the same fault system does suggest a possible connection which would bear more detailed investigation.

Dynamic conditions. Most evidence, including published earthquake records, suggests that the advances were not due to any pervasive external cause but were the result of unstable dynamic conditions in the particular glacier systems. The mechanism indicated is that of an ice "reservoir" forming in the middle portion of each glacier and being filled over a period of years with ice which flows in from tributaries while the stagnant lower terminal portion of the glacier is being reduced by ablation. When certain critical conditions are reached the glacier becomes unstable and a sudden brief movement of the ice takes place. This movement so depletes the reservoir area that when the ice comes to rest virtual stagnation occurs in the lower glacier and the process is repeated. . . .

APPENDIX E

AIR SUPPLY

EXPEDITIONS into these mountains have been made without air support, but when time is short and a journey of some duration is to be made this support is essential. It is merely another method of porterage.

One supply drop may now be made, in McKinley Park, to any expedition, scientific or not. Outside its borders there are no restrictions. The Park authorities may allow more drops if the expedition has scientific aims.

The use of aircraft is, however, expensive. The cost of chartering a civil pilot and aircraft to fly in a four-man party with a thousand pounds of food and equipment from McKinley Park Station to McGonagall Pass is just over £ 170. The round trip takes two hours' flying time, and each load consists of one man and 100 pounds of freight, or equivalent weight. The tariff is $40 or approximately £ 14 5s., an hour.

It is extremely unlikely that the United States Air Force would consider supporting a civilian party, although they might supply rescue cover. Alternatively this latter requirement is sometimes undertaken by members of the Alaskan Alpine Club which has its headquarters in Fairbanks.

APPENDIX F

DIVISION OF PLANNING RESPONSIBILITY

TASK	PERSON RESPONSIBLE
1. *POLICY* a) Application to W.O.* b) Transportation c) Air rescue cover d) High-altitude boots e) W.D. clothing f) Ordering of W.D. food g) Application for funds h) Financial backing i) Provision of sledge j) Negotiations with U.S.A.F.	Capt. Mills
2. *EQUIPMENT* a) Purchase and reassembly of equipment b) Return of equipment c) Film and camera d) Meteorological equipment e) All W.D. clothing f) Fitness of all equipment for use g) Design and provision of expedition flag h) Provision of route flags	Lieut. Pritchard
3. *MEDICAL AND RATIONS* a) Provision of all medical supplies b) Provision of all foods—except W.D. c) Inoculations and vaccinations d) Certificates of fitness for members e) W.D. food—collection only f) Biscuits (hard) 30 lb.	Capt. Kinloch Capt. Deacock
4. *FINANCE* a) Maintenance of accounts b) Application for dollars c) Insurance of certain items of equipment d) Customs clearance	Capt. Deacock
5. *STORAGE AND PACKING* a) Listing of equipment b) Provision of labels, etc. c) Storage d) Provision of packing materials e) Packing	Capt. Deacock

APPENDIX G

FINANCIAL STATEMENT

INCOME	£	s.	d.
Members' initial contribution	500	0	0
Members' last expedition contribution	18	0	0
Mount Everest Foundation	350	0	0
Publishers	319	10	0
Insurance	278	0	9
Daily Telegraph (photos)	6	15	0
(1) Checks from members	33	16	10
Sale of camera	110	0	0
Parachute Brigade Mountaineering Club	30	0	0
$50 gift Dawson Creek	17	17	2
Sale of photo, Mobiloil	10	10	0
	£1,675	16	10

EXPENDITURE	£	s.	d.
Equipment and clothing	214	3	8
Films	93	7	11
Camera	100	0	0
Food	20	10	4
Travel	619	15	0
Insurance (premium pers.)	51	1	0
Travelers checks (cash)	50	0	0
(2) Transfer to $	450	0	8
Postage, stationery, cables, etc.	3	18	8
Post expedition expenses:			
Color slides	20	10	0
Printing and enlarging photographs	10	0	0
Typing agency	18	0	0
Sundry expenses	24	10	3
	£1,675	16	10

257

INCOME

(2) Sterling transfer to $ (£450)	1,260	00
Book option (U.S.)	265	00
	1,525	00
	1,525	00

EXPENDITURE

P.A.A. excess baggage	85	50
C.N.R. fares	250	60
C.P.A. excess baggage	153	09
Grand Hotel (Ottawa)	21	
Return fares CNR/CPA	240	
P.A.A. excess baggage	43	82
Officers' mess, Ladd A.F.B.	28	35
P.A.A.	154	
A. G. Harris (exchange)	100	
Greek Line expenses	50	
Photographic equipment	48	
Personal cash issue on journey	50	
U.S.A.F. entertainment grant	30	
(1) Personal cash loans	94	50
Sundry expenses (including food on journey and camera hire)	175	50
	1,524	36
		64
	1,525	00

Balance as at July 25, 1956: $ 00 64.

Note: It is doubtful that the expedition expenses could have been reduced. The fare accounts for almost two-thirds of the total cost, and with the pound comparing so unfavorably with the dollar, all other expenses in North America are very high. Without British Army, Canadian, and U.S.A.F. help the cost of the expedition might well have been prohibitive.

GLOSSARY

Abseil. To descend by means of a rope.

Anorak hood. Hood or windproof jacket.

Balaclava helmet. Woolen helmet which covers all of head and neck except face.

Belay. To secure another climber by hitching the rope around ice axe, oneself, etc.

Bergschrund. A large crevasse where a glacier separates from the mountain wall.

Cirque. A steep hollow like an amphitheater in a mountainside.

Col. A pass between peaks.

Couloir. A mountainside gorge.

Crampons. Steel spikes on a framework which can be attached to one's boots.

Crevasse. An opening where under stress glacial ice has cracked.

Gendarme. A rock tower.

Glissade. A descent by sliding.

Hummock. A ridge of ice.

Ice axe. A tool having both a point and a pick.

Ice fall. A steep drop in a glacier, badly broken.

Karabiner. A snap ring.

Leading through. Changing the leader on a climbing rope after each pitch, the second man climbing past the first.

Massif. The main block or mass of a mountain.

Moraine. Rock and other debris carried down by a glacier.

Pitch. A short, steep rise.

Piton. A metal spike designed to hold when driven into rock or ice.

Prusik loop. A loop tied to a rope by a prusik knot. When not under pressure the loop may be moved at will up and down the main rope.

Sérac. An upthrust ice tower.

Tarbuck knot. A knot which contracts under strain, reducing direct stress on the rope. Used for tying climbers onto climbing rope.

Traverse. A crossing from side to side.

Tump line. A line or strap which is attached to a load and is passed round the forehead.